Advance praise for *Achieve Brand Integrity*

"Achieving Brand Integrity is critical to the long-term success of any company. Having every person throughout an organization living and breathing what the brand is about is essential for this to happen. Brand Integrity Inc. enables all employees in a company to be aligned around one common vision and how it is accomplished."

— Colleen Wegman

PRESIDENT, WEGMANS FOOD MARKETS

"I have met many people during my career who believe they know how to build a successful corporate branding program. Gregg and the Brand Integrity team are simply the best and I guarantee you will adopt some of their ideas in this book."

— Arunas Chesonis

CHAIRMAN AND CHIEF EXECUTIVE OFFICER, PAETEC COMMUNICATIONS, INC.

"*Achieve Brand Integrity* provides a culture management framework and incredibly useful tools to help a company define who it is and where it is heading. Most important, this book will get you started thinking through the employee behaviors and company experiences necessary to get you there."

— Mark Erickson

CHIEF OPERATING OFFICER, ERICKSON RETIREMENT COMMUNITIES

"A branding program sets the direction for a company to pursue. Any book that describes how to get employees heading in that direction is worth reading. *Achieve Brand Integrity* is just such a book."

— Jack Trout

AUTHOR OF *DIFFERENTIATE OR DIE: SURVIVAL IN OUR ERA OF KILLER COMPETITION* AND *TROUT ON STRATEGY*

"The ultimate validation of the Achieving Brand Integrity methodology shows in the remarkable success of the companies that have taken the lessons most to heart. We are honored to have Gregg Lederman as an alum, teaching this methodology at Simon."

— Mark Zupan

DEAN, WILLIAM E. SIMON GRADUATE SCHOOL OF BUSINESS ADMINISTRATION, UNIVERSITY OF ROCHESTER

ACHIEVE BRAND INTEGRITY

ACHIEVE

Ten Truths You Must Know to

BRAND

Enhance Employee Performance and

INTEGRITY

Increase Company Profits

Gregg Lederman

PRESS

Rochester, New York

B@W Press
60 Park Avenue
Rochester, NY 14607

Design, layout, and illustrations by James Wondrack
Author photograph by Walter Colley
Indexed by Clive Pyne Book Indexing Services

Library of Congress Catalog Number: 2007902987

ISBN-13: 978-0-9795875-0-4
ISBN-10: 0-9795875-0-6

Printed in the United States of America

For bulk sales please contact:
B@W Press
60 Park Avenue
Rochester, New York 14607
585-442-5404

Dedication

In writing *Achieve Brand Integrity,* I was fortunate enough to have access to the wisdom and understanding of many people, including my wife and kids, the team at Brand Integrity Inc., Wondrack Design Inc., Potential Point LLC, and the leaders and employees of Brand Integrity's clients.

To my family: Karyn, Caroline, Katie, and Lucy, thank you for your support, patience, and endless love as I traveled the journey of writing this book.

To the Brand Integrity Team: Thank you for your continuous inspiration, ideas, and passion for enhancing the Achieving Brand Integrity process.

To our clients: Thank you for your continued efforts towards Achieving Brand Integrity. Your dedication to our process has enabled us to grow and help other organizations.

"David, based on our new employee
performance program, you actually OWE
the company $2,000 dollars."

Table of Contents

Preface

Brand Integrity Inc. is a brand strategy practice group that specializes in employee performance. The firm is based in Rochester, New York. Brand Integrity Inc. has helped some of the best companies in America to develop strategies and programs that have enabled them to make millions of dollars in new sales, build tremendous loyalty among their employees and customers, and drive culture transformation throughout their organizations — culture change that has dramatically increased employee morale and productivity.

Achieve Brand Integrity is the first-ever "how-to" book to define for business leaders what a brand strategy is and how to use it to deliver actionable results. The content is based on the firm's experiences working with hundreds of companies ranging in size from $6 million to $20 billion. It is also the framework for the brand strategy course Gregg teaches as an adjunct faculty member to second-year MBA students at the University of Rochester's William E. Simon School of Business Administration.

1

Introduction

Our company has an incredibly efficient, productive, and profit-focused brand-building process — *Achieving Brand Integrity®*. As a concept, *Brand Integrity* is both journey and destination.

• The journey is a strategy-building exercise for business leaders and their teams.

• The destination is a powerful brand.

• Brand Integrity is the point when your company is known as who and what you say you are while reaching business goals — when all of your marketing messages and sales-speak are backed up and delivered upon.

Simply stated, you've achieved *Brand Integrity* when your company *is* who and what it says it is!

In this book, I will share with you the ten Truths about branding that drive the success of the *Achieving Brand Integrity* process — truths that you can apply to your own company. Truths that, applied in the development and implementation of a brand strategy, will drive the three results you're looking for: increased employee productivity, enhanced customer loyalty, and new sales.

This book is packed with energy, knowledge, and humor (what an incredible combination!) to teach and inspire business leaders and their employees.

3

THIS IS A BOOK FOR LEADERS

This book is written for business leaders. It is *not* for mid-level managers who do not aspire to eventually play a leading role in a company. Why? Because business leaders are the only ones who can truly invest in and successfully execute a profit-driving brand strategy.

This book is written in a conversational style. I use real language that is used by real business leaders in companies today. I have tried to cut out all of the MBA jargon and typical business lingo.

YOU NEED THIS BOOK

You may be thinking, "Why does the world need another book about branding?" Type "branding" as a keyword on Amazon.com, and hundreds of titles appear (614 last time I checked).

Trust me, this book is different. I will not regurgitate the same old rhetoric you've read in previous branding books. Instead, I will provide how-to examples and access to tools and techniques for actually doing the work discussed throughout the book.

As a business leader, you need this book so that you can quit throwing money at your brand. Quit trying to shape your brand through costly and ineffective marketing and advertising. You need it so you can start *living* your brand through your people and the work processes and experiences that make your company different. Not only different, but better than the competition.

Leaders who work for companies that spend too much money and people time on marketing strategies and tactics with little or nothing to show for it are confused regarding *what* their brand is, *why* it matters, and *how* to manage it. They just can't seem to get away from a marketing mentality when it comes to thinking about their brand and how to leverage it in the marketplace. Many don't realize that the marketing department cannot control and manage the brand on their own. In Truth #5: *Marketing and Advertising Can Kill Your Brand*, I'll give you some background on costly mistakes that companies have made while trying to build brand awareness and loyalty and instead only created customer recall without tangible results.

4

Are you asking, "What is a brand?" Well, read on, my friend. This is one of the few places you'll actually realize what it means to have a great brand. I'll give you not just a solid definition of brand, but also the first-ever definition of a brand strategy **for business leaders.**

THIS IS A BOOK ABOUT ORGANIZATIONAL BRANDING, NOT PRODUCT POSITIONING

There are two pervasive types of brand-building in today's business world.

1. Product branding (a.k.a., positioning).

2. Organizational branding (a.k.a., culture transformation and business strategy).

This book focuses on how to build a brand strategy at the organizational level. For companies where the brand *is* the business strategy, people need to buy in to it in order to make sure it's understood, committed to, and executed upon. Those of you who think you need a book on product branding, I encourage you to read this book anyway, keeping in mind that a product has personality, attributes, and associations that drive brand success just as an organization does. You will find the principles, processes, and insights shared in this book can be safely applied to a product strategy. However, the examples used will be focused on the organization, not products and services.

You know how little it helps to build a brand with pithy marketing messages and catchy taglines. Wouldn't you rather figure out a way to align everyone in your organization so that everything they do helps build your company's reputation? Wouldn't it be nice to have all employees focused on the same actionable strategy? Most leaders are all too familiar with brand-building through advertising yet have limited experience with brand-building from a people and process perspective. It has been the experience of the team at Brand Integrity that most leaders are somewhat confused yet intrigued to learn more. I hope you're one of them.

A decade ago, the rules were different. You could build customer loyalty through great service and brand awareness campaigns. Today, advertising is a sure-fire way to kill a bad product. Consumer expectations, with respect to product and service delivery, have skyrocketed and competition in almost all industry segments has intensified. Customers expect you to delight them with your offering. If you don't, it's much easier for them to switch to another brand. As easy as clicking a mouse, most of the time. Lower switching costs for consumers and fewer barriers-to-entry for your competition make succeeding in business more difficult than ever before.

You need to do more than determine and advertise your brand's *point of difference.* You need to define your company's uniqueness, align it with the market, and motivate your people to deliver upon it. This is the key difference between organizational and product branding. In product branding, your product does the talking with the way it operates and the benefits it delivers. With respect to organizational branding, the people (your employees) make it happen.

Forget about marketing and advertising for now. To achieve *Brand Integrity*, all of your employees must follow well-defined processes and systems. I will demonstrate how implementation by employees is the driving force behind the execution of a successful brand strategy.

How to read this book

This book is organized by Truths
Each chapter provides a Truth that will guide you through the brand strategy process.

This book is about action
There are no chapter conclusions restating the important points. All of the points are important. Each chapter recommends actions to take in order to *do* the strategic ideas presented.

Brand challenge

"My own leadership team is not on the same page — doesn't share the same vision of what success looks like."

THIS BOOK IS WEB-BASED

Most chapters are accompanied by online tools and techniques that are **free**. You'll find tons of valuable tools and directions on how to use them. All you have to do is go to www.brandintegrity.com and get them.

THIS BOOK HAS SOLUTIONS

In the margins, I call out a few of the most noted branding challenges faced in business today. The good news is that I've provided solutions to all of them.

THIS BOOK IS ABOUT CONSISTENCY

In Truth #1, I provide insights about our friend, the Consistency King. Consistency is so important in the brand-building process that we always tell clients "consistency is king" (or queen). So the

Consistency King will appear throughout the book as a continual reminder that if you want to develop a strong brand for your company, then employees must be in a position to consistently deliver results for customers. Consistency is the key to brand-building success. Therefore, I will ensure you get a consistent dose of the Consistency King. (No, this is not the Burger King king.)

"Consistency is king."

THIS BOOK IS PROFITABLE

There are three things most business leaders have in common: they want productive employees, loyal customers, and more sales. There is one thing **all** business leaders want: more profits.

This book shows you how to get more profits. You'll learn proven approaches to build brand strategies that will take you miles beyond the over-simplistic building of company values, mission and vision statements, and other relatively useless bulletin board material. A company mission is nice to have if your employees know how to do it every day. You will learn a more strategic approach that will bring your values, mission, and vision to life!

SOLUTION

"Bring a group of leaders together to create a shared vision — a clear picture of who you are, what you do, and why customers care."

THIS BOOK IS WRITTEN BY ME BUT CONTAINS A LOT OF "WE"

The tools, techniques, and content about the *Achieving Brand Integrity* process are communicated by me. But the insights and logic were developed over the past decade by my team and me at Brand Integrity Inc. One client at a time, we have been able to glean innovative ways to deliver results that have helped our clients to enhance employee performance and increase company profits. Our clients continue to rave about the *Achieving Brand Integrity* process and they believe in following the ten Truths.

Read on to learn why ...

Introduction

Achieve
Brand
Integrity

9

Truth
NUMBER

A Brand Strategy Is the Ultimate Business Strategy and Often the Least Understood

Truth
NUMBER

1

A Brand
Strategy Is
the Ultimate
Business
Strategy
and Often
the Least
Understood

TOPICS

IDEAS ····⟩ ACTION

---

1 Develop Top
  Business
  Objectives

11

Truth
NUMBER

1

A Brand
Strategy Is
the Ultimate
Business
Strategy
and Often
the Least
Understood

Buckman's Bakery & Ice Cream has been a landmark in Rochester, NY, since 1914 when it became the first dairy in the market. In the 1950s it became Rochester's premier bakery. In the 1970s, Buckman's was the local destination for homemade, old-fashioned ice cream. People had come to know Buckman's as the home of the best cakes, pies, donuts, and ice cream. It was a family event to take a trip to Buckman's. By the 1990s, perceptions of Buckman's had dramatically changed. Over the course of ten to fifteen years, the market was infiltrated with competition on all fronts. Ice cream parlors, donut shops, bagel bakeries, and supermarkets were competing with Buckman's.

Buckman's had lost its uniqueness. It was no longer the premier anything as far as the quality of products or the manner in which they were delivered to customers.

In the early 1990s, Buckman's was on the verge of bankruptcy. I, along with my business partner Tim Vottis, saw an opportunity. We scouted the establishment for several weeks and were shocked to see 7,000+ square feet of pure filth. But even more alarming were the staff — generally lazy, unkempt, rude, and careless — delivering bad experiences, one customer at a time. Amazingly, some customers still frequented Buckman's.

During our research into the viability of the bakery, we discovered a nostalgic feeling that customers associated with Buckman's — a feeling they wanted to share with new generations despite the current state of the business. The business seemed oblivious to customers' desire for a meaningful experience, and was losing upwards of $15,000 per month. And the current owner wanted out.

Tim and I jumped at the chance to rebuild Buckman's Bakery & Ice Cream. We understood the power of perceptions. We knew that if we could change the customer experience, we could take it back to the days when Buckman's was a thriving destination for local families to share milkshakes and pies. We could bring back the flair that once made Buckman's a special place in the hearts and minds of Rochesterians. We could bring back customers.

What we accomplished wasn't rocket science, but it sure worked.

First, we established a vision for the future and a list of behavioral guidelines that we would use to hold staff accountable for bringing the vision to life. On our first day, we handed out the guidelines for success to all of the past workers. All but a few of the 30 employees who had been with the company stayed with us.

Not surprisingly, only three made it through the first year. Why? Because visions are easy to talk about, but behaviors demand accountability.

> Truth #6: *Behaviors and Experiences Make the Invisible Visible* will share an approach for positioning your company to develop visible, objective, and easily measured behaviors to ensure your brand is delivered by employees throughout your company.

Next, we decreased the product assortment to eliminate the ones that Tim (our expert baker) couldn't guarantee would always be great. Gone were the cakes, pies, breads, and pastries once considered staples for Buckman's customers. Instead, we became great at making donuts, muffins, and ice cream. Three core products were all that we needed to up the value of the business ten-fold in a few short years.

Finally, we set performance expectations for staff and held them accountable for results. For instance, the second time you saw a customer, you would ask their name and try to remember what they ordered. Remembering people and their preferences was part of the job description. You either did it or you were out.

We hired great people and established reasonable behavioral and experiential expectations. In doing so, employees became accountable to us and to each other. And, they liked working in an environment where accountability was valued.

Truth
NUMBER

1

A Brand
Strategy Is
the Ultimate
Business
Strategy
and Often
the Least
Understood

In the more than three years Tim and I ran Buckman's, we never had to post a job opening for a customer service position. Our staff became so loyal to our approach of defining expectations and ensuring accountability that they would refer our best leads. Staff would never recommend friends who wouldn't be good workers (the kiss of death for most minimum wage/fast food employers) for they knew they would be held accountable to our "You're Both Fired" policy. We worked hard to develop great employees. If they wanted us to hire a friend, then that friend needed to be as great at keeping the store clean and the customers happy as they were. Simple and effective!

Truth
NUMBER

1

A Brand Strategy Is the Ultimate Business Strategy and Often the Least Understood

Keep in mind, our employees were mostly minimum wage (or close) workers. Why were we able to attract and keep dedicated employees when our competition was struggling to find any help at all? Because we re-established the Buckman's Brand from the inside out. We defined our vision and made it meaningful to our employees by providing visible, measurable behaviors. We provided systems and approaches for delighting customers, and they liked it. They enjoyed contributing to the success of an organization they believed in.

Over time, customers began to talk. The positive perceptions about Buckman's were coming alive again. Yes, some customers were upset about the limited product assortment and we did get our fair share of complaints early on. But as time passed, customers began to focus on the clean store and the energetic and friendly employees. Customers began to appreciate consistent quality and being treated with care and respect. They loved being remembered every time they came in. They loved the Buckman's Experience!

Tim and I sold Buckman's for ten times what we paid for it after just three short years. Today, people still ask me what our secret was. I tell them the three things we did really well:

1. We hired the best people.

2. We produced only products we could be great at (less was much more).

3. We established a performance-based work culture where minimum wage employees expected to be — and appreciated being — accountable for keeping the store clean and delighting customers at every point of interaction.

At the time, I didn't realize that our recipe for success at Buckman's would be the foundation of what I believe is the world's greatest brand strategy development process — the *Achieving Brand Integrity* process that is grounded in the philosophy that perceptions are created and managed by the reality your company delivers with its products and services.

Whether you, as a leader in a company, are building product brands or an organization-wide brand, you need to follow a process for creating and managing the perceptions of your customers. Most of the time when we think about a product, we think about what we like, how it makes us feel, and the results of using it. The product begins to take on a personality of its own in our minds. Much is the same for an organization. However, orchestrating the experiences and executing them in ways that lead to a compelling personality for the company is a lot more challenging than doing so for a product.

The Truths outlined in this book will take you through the brand-building methodology Brand Integrity Inc. uses for helping clients discover who their organization is, what benefits they can deliver to customers, and a plan for how to do it. This is the *Achieving Brand Integrity* process, with *Brand Integrity* being the point at which you are who you say you are while reaching desired business goals.

1.1 THE EVOLUTION OF THE CONCEPT CALLED BRAND

Let's begin with branding. Branding is one of today's most overused and abused buzzwords. Business leaders everywhere have become obsessed with the idea of branding their companies. There are currently more than 4,000 books, articles, and Web sites that discuss the topic of branding. Every management consultant; ad agency; and Tom, Dick, and Harry uses the term "branding," yet many have little to no understanding of what a brand is or how to go about branding their organization.

15

Branding is one of today's most overused and abused buzzwords.

Truth
NUMBER

1

A Brand
Strategy Is
the Ultimate
Business
Strategy
and Often
the Least
Understood

The term "branding" dates back to days of the Wild West when cattle ranchers would put an indelible mark on their livestock to stake their claim. Like the cattle ranchers, companies today attempt to brand themselves and their products or services, *hoping* to leave lasting impressions that will influence customer thoughts and actions. However, creating the brand is the easy part. Managing the perceptions of that brand is considerably more difficult.

Everyone's talking about brand, because in today's competitive market, it's the most important ingredient for success.

A strong brand is the end result of a good business strategy that is executed thoughtfully and **consistently**.

"We give great customer service!"

"I hope you think you got great customer service."

The strength of your brand over time depends on how well you can align the people and processes behind it. And building alignment is hard work! Once you've organized your brand strategy, use it for the blueprint for growth including such elements as:

- product and service development
- leadership and human resource practices
- operational procedures and policies
- vendor and partner relationships
- employee loyalty
- company culture

When challenged at cocktail parties by myopic business leaders who believe (falsely) that they are in a commodity business where low price wins, I have to defend the concept of brand. I usually ask, "Are you really in a commodity business, extracting a commodity in the form of a raw material?" (Only once has the answer to this been yes, and then I delivered my Morton Salt example, which I'll share with you in a moment.)

Then, I'll ask these questions to better understand the value of a more powerful brand for their particular business:

Truth
NUMBER

1

A Brand
Strategy Is
the Ultimate
Business
Strategy
and Often
the Least
Understood

1. Can your company deliver a product or service offering in a unique way? What's different about the way the product is created, distributed, or serviced when compared to how your competition does it?

2. Could you charge a different price in a different way from your competition?

3. Is your company better than the competition at understanding the needs and wants of customers and fulfilling those needs and wants?

The answer to all three questions is typically a resounding *yes* because most businesses can deliver their products and services in unique ways that help make them **different** (unlike a commodity).

Most companies produce goods and services. However, virtually all companies deliver them through people and operational processes that enable differentiation. So if you are going to build a brand strategy that truly makes your company different while enhancing productivity of your people and profitability of your company, you will need to stay focused on managing your people and your processes.

The potential: stronger competitive advantage through meaningful customer experiences, more premium pricing, and a more relevant offering that is better aligned with the needs and wants of customers.

Case in point: Coffee was once viewed as a commodity ... until Starbucks created an entire experience around the product and

17

the way it is priced and delivered. Today, millions of people have no problem going to "Fourbucks" (ahem, I mean Starbucks) Coffee for an iced beverage. Unbelievably, large amounts of people (like me) will even drop twenty or more dollars on a ridiculously overpriced travel coffee mug. Why? Because of the friendly service, enjoyable music, and variety of caffeinated beverages to choose from.

Now, back to Morton Salt. Salt is most definitely a commodity. When handed a salt shaker, you don't think about what type of salt you are adding to your soup nor can you taste the difference. So why would any smart consumer choose to pay a 10 percent premium for Morton Salt versus the private-label brand? At the time of this writing, Morton Salt was sold at my local grocery store for 99 cents, compared to the local competitor at 89 cents.

Hmm … it's only a dime more. Why not go with the brand name I think I can trust?

"Please pass the Morton's."

Okay, here come the obligatory definitions of brand. They provide powerful insights and are certainly in alignment with the ten Truths about branding described throughout this book.

These definitions are high level and will need further breakdown to make them more meaningful to customers and employees of your company.

1.2 A Few Definitions of Brand

1. DEFINITION OF BRAND FOR THE MASSES (ALL PEOPLE IN BUSINESS)

A brand is the sum total of every experience a customer has with your company and its products and services — a sum total that customers begin to think of as the promise you make.

The experiences delivered by your company through its people and processes are what make you different from your competition. The experiences that are meaningful to your customers provide your competitive advantage.

2. DEFINITION OF BRAND FOR EMPLOYEES

A brand is the sum total of workplace experiences an employee has with your company. When an employee lives and breathes your brand at work, he or she is more productive. And so, more profitable.

3. DEFINITION OF BRAND FOR CUSTOMERS

A brand is the sum total of experiences a customer has with your company. These experiences lead the customer to connect with your organization, its people, and its products and services on an emotional and rational level, increasing the likelihood that they will buy more stuff[1] from your company.

1.3 The First-ever Definition of Brand Strategy

Okay, so simply what is a brand strategy? You've been quite patient, so here we go. The first-ever definition that remains true across continents, countries, markets, industries, and even in *your very own company*:

A BRAND STRATEGY IS ...
THE PROCESS OF ALIGNING WHAT WE SAY WITH WHAT WE DO, TO POSITIVELY INFLUENCE WHAT CUSTOMERS THINK.

"We" refers to your company. "Customers" include your company's employees, partners, stockholders, competitors, and anyone else whose positive perceptions will enhance productivity and profits.

Truth
NUMBER

1

A Brand Strategy Is the Ultimate Business Strategy and Often the Least Understood

1 Stuff: Products and services your company sells that you want customers to buy more of.

19

WHAT WE SAY	WHAT WE DO	WHAT THEY THINK

Truth
NUMBER

1

A Brand
Strategy Is
the Ultimate
Business
Strategy
and Often
the Least
Understood

"Team, we deliver great service, quickly!"	*"Sorry, we can't possibly ..."*	*"Boy, their service is slow!"*

Pretty simple, isn't it? Pretty powerful, too. Powerful in that a brand strategy aligns your entire company around a shared vision that includes actionable initiatives for success.

Creating the brand strategy may seem like the easy part. For some companies it is; for most, it isn't. Either way, implementing it effectively and efficiently is what helps great companies stand apart from good companies.

> Truth #6: *Behaviors and Experiences Make the Invisible Visible* will take you through the process of creating a brand strategy.

1.4 Branding: Self-help for Businesses

In an article entitled "Obsessive Branding Disorder" in the October 2005 issue of *Fast Company* magazine, author Lucas Conley shares a unique and valid perspective on branding and the hype around it. Conley refers to branding as "The self-help industry of corporate America." He brings to light the point that executives in business today are obsessed with the idea of branding their organizations. However, they don't seem to see that branding without the hype is nothing more than "commonsense strategy." Conley refers to branding as Business 101. He states, "Run a good business and your brand will follow."

As simplified as this may sound, it's true! Branding can be quite simple in concept, yet very challenging to actually implement well.

Is it fair to say that experiences are what drive perceptions about your company? You bet it is. The fact is that **90 percent of the time, individuals will judge your company by the experience they or someone they know has with your brand and only 10 percent or less by the marketing messages they've heard**. If this is the case (and it is), then why do so many companies exhaust ungodly amounts of resources into pretentious marketing messages focused on *saying* the strategy and invest so little in the management of *doing* the strategy?

Truth
NUMBER
1
A Brand
Strategy Is
the Ultimate
Business
Strategy
and Often
the Least
Understood

The answer: Because branding is falsely viewed as only a marketing discipline in which perceptions are thought to be reality, as opposed to a business strategy in which reality (what you actually deliver) drives perceptions. This concept may alter the way you say one of the most over-abused statements: "perception is reality." In the business world, reality is perception. Please hang on to this premise as you continue your journey through this book.

"Come eat at Doug's. We have friendly service and great-tasting food."

"Wow, they're really friendly at Bob's. And the food was great."

"Yeah, no wonder they're so busy."

21

Ninety percent of the time, individuals will judge your company by the experience they or someone they know has with your brand and only 10 percent or less by the marketing messages they've heard.

Truth
NUMBER

1

A Brand
Strategy Is
the Ultimate
Business
Strategy
and Often
the Least
Understood

1.5 The Four Realities of Branding

Does your company lack strategic direction? Does the path you've set change with the wind based on the hidden agendas of your leaders or market and competitive fluctuations? If so, and you're frustrated enough, it might be time to consider a different approach. A brand strategy might be just what you're looking for. In order to understand the true potential of a brand strategy, you must start with understanding the Four Realities of Branding. These realities, once understood, have the power to help you ensure successful implementation of your company's strategic and operational goals and objectives.

FIRST REALITY OF BRANDING: THE BRAND IS NOT A PART OF THE BUSINESS, IT IS THE BUSINESS

According to *Spirit* magazine, in 2004 Southwest Airlines took in almost 225,895 applications for 1,706 positions. Do you think it was able to be selective and ensure that it hired only the best, highest potential performers who really fit the company's culture? Do you think Southwest had a clear vision for success with stated principles and values for people to strive for each day? It sure did. Leaders at Southwest approach their business from a brand strategy perspective. They've been doing it for years and continue to profit from it. Luckily for Southwest, only a few in its industry even have the capability to try to compete.

The fact is that every employee interaction within your company impacts the brand. And there are lots of these interactions! Each one makes it either easier or harder for you to keep and recruit great people and good customers. These interactions directly affect costs of payroll and customer sales, which dramatically influence cash flow for operations.

The most successful, future-looking companies (whether large household names or privately held neighborhood shops) recognize that the brand *is* the playing field for the game of business.

SECOND REALITY OF BRANDING: A BRAND IS ABOUT EXPERIENCES, NOT LOGOS AND TAGLINES

At this point in the book, I hope you're not thinking of your company's brand as a logo or tagline-type message.

Your brand is made up of concepts that go well beyond logos, posters, and mouse pads that you may be tempted to hand out and post around the office (or maybe you already have). Your brand is more of a people strategy than a marketing strategy. Since this is true, it is obviously fair to say that the brand strategy should not be developed or "siloed" in the marketing department. So the next time you get a call from someone with a question about your brand, do *not* pass them on to marketing department personnel.

Truth
NUMBER

1

A Brand
Strategy Is
the Ultimate
Business
Strategy
and Often
the Least
Understood

If a brand was nothing more than a logo or tagline, any one of these could be used by your company and called a brand strategy. By the way, I heard Phil Knight originally paid $35 for his Nike logo.

Remember, the purpose of a brand strategy is to influence what people think about your company in ways that cause them to take the action your company is looking for and the only way to influence what people think is to manage the consistent execution of employee behaviors that will drive customer experiences.

The purpose of a brand strategy
is to influence what people think.

Truth
NUMBER

1

A Brand
Strategy Is
the Ultimate
Business
Strategy
and Often
the Least
Understood

There are three primary actions that your brand will stimulate in customers. Unfortunately, two of them won't help you grow your business more profitably. (When reading the three, consider the relevance to employees as well as to customers.)

CUSTOMER RESPONSES TO YOUR BRAND

1. Your brand and its associated experiences are not what a customer is looking for so they decide **not to do business** with your company.

2. The customer is not sure if your company and its products are right for them, so they take no action; **they don't buy your stuff.**

3. The customer finds that your company and products are a good fit for them, so they decide to **buy from you.**

BINGO! You win! Stay consistent with the experience and you're likely to never lose that customer. They may even become brand

OUR MARKETING DEPARTMENT (employees)	OUR UNPAID MARKETING DEPARTMENT (customers)

"Our customer service is incredible."	*"Yeah, we deliver like no other."*	*"Their service is really incredible. I love doing business with them."*	*"I agree. My cousin referred them to me."*

ambassadors for your company and its products and services by telling others about their positive experiences. Before you know it, you will have your own unpaid marketing department — a sign of a truly strong brand.

This is the part of the book where the myopic marketing employee gets nervous about their "awareness campaign" budget being repurposed into activities that will actually drive employee behaviors and customer experiences. This marketing person hopes their CEO doesn't read these realities about branding. This person has already ditched this book.

MARKETING DIRECTOR

"I hope they don't take money from my marketing budget."

THIRD REALITY OF BRANDING: THE LITTLE THINGS THAT YOU DO CONSISTENTLY ARE MUCH MORE IMPORTANT THAN THE BIG THINGS YOU SAY!

No one is really listening when you tell them how your company is the industry leader in "blah, blah, blah." Or that you are experts in delivering "blah, blah," and are known for incredibly high-quality "blah." Even if you think they're listening to your salespeople or advertising message, do you really think they're *hearing it*? Don't count on it!

What your target audience may be listening to are your customer testimonials. They'll probably pay a lot more attention to what their friends, relatives, or colleagues say about your product. You see, those people are much more believable than you or anyone in your company.

"Blah, blah, blah."   "Who cut this guy's hair?"   "Did I turn off the iron?"   "Do I have food in my teeth?"

As consumers we are bombarded with endless messages, broken promises, and facts and figures on a daily basis. How could we possibly process all of the information, keep the facts straight, and formulate accurate opinions that will help us make the best choices?

When we have an experience or hear about someone else's, our emotional and logical receptors are instantly tuned up and ready to process the information. Not only process it, but store it, prioritize it, and use it to make buying decisions. And buying decisions are what you want for your company.

If people judge a company by the experience they or someone else has, then why do so many companies still waste outrageous amounts of money on advertising and "marcomm" tactics? Why don't they focus on the experiences that are most relevant to their target customers? The fact is that all companies want customers to believe certain things about them and their products. If you want them to believe, they need reasons to believe. Well-planned and executed experiences provide those reasons.

BRAND CHALLENGE

"We tell customers and prospects over and over again and they don't seem to believe us."

The reality is that they will see it when they believe it. Show the customer. Don't tell him. Show him through an experience that is relevant.

Stop throwing away your marketing dollars!

REMEMBER, CONSISTENCY IS KING!

A colleague, Patrick Ahern, and I were recently meeting with a prospective client. We were asking a lot of questions about his business, the challenges he was currently facing, and the solutions he had in mind. Naturally, this prospect wanted to learn more about Brand Integrity Inc. and our thoughts on branding. After about an hour together sharing business philosophies and demonstrating how smart and successful we all are, he asked "If there is one thing that I need to take away from this meeting about brand-building, what would it be?" Patrick and I looked at him a bit perplexed. His question was so simple. We were both shocked that we had not been asked it before. He pressed on, "What is the one thing that matters most to ensure that a company can build its brand to drive profits? Is there one thing?"

SOLUTION

"Use testimonials and more proactively provide references. These are way more believable than you or your employees."

Patrick and I looked at each other and back at the prospect. Then we each got out a piece of paper and wrote that one thing down. Both of us passed our papers to the prospect and sure enough (luckily), we had written not only the same idea, but the exact same word: *consistency*. While Patrick and I had never discussed that particular question, we are both schooled in the principles that power brand-building. When you add up all the countless insights and information available on brand-building, you can sum up in one word what will drive success — consistency.

"Consistency
is king."

If you want to be known for something, then deliver that something consistently. We tell clients all the time, don't be great sometimes and okay other times. Just be good all the time and you will have much greater success. As human beings, we need consistency. From the time we are kids, we rely on a structured, consistent agenda to thrive. Try to take a 3-year-old out of her daily routine. Take her to the movies or the mall at nap time. Ouch! Okay, don't try it, just trust me; I have three little girls. Adults are no different. We all want to know what to expect. Of course, if you can be *great* all the time, go for it.

Think back to the example of my first company, Buckman's. We followed this example of being consistently good by ensuring that employees understood behavioral expectations. At the highest of levels, behaviors must be established that can then be tailored to each job in the company.

I believe in the philosophy behind Jim Collins' widely successful book *Good to Great*. Good is the enemy of great. However, consistently being *good* can enable your company to be much more profitable than being only occasionally *great*.

The reality: You're better off doing a few things well all of the time than doing a lot of things mediocre some of the time.

Fourth Reality of Branding: A brand strategy is the single most important differentiator between a good company and a great company

Great companies have people and processes that make them great.

For any company in any industry, this fact remains true: your competition cannot easily replicate your people (human capital) or processes (quality assurance, innovation, customer service, etc.). They can (and probably will) copy your marketing message, but they will not be able to consistently deliver the same experiences without your people and processes. Since this is the case, why don't more companies focus their energy on talent management and process improvement? Maybe because doing so is less sexy than focusing on sales-driven marketing initiatives.

Truth
NUMBER

1

A Brand
Strategy Is
the Ultimate
Business
Strategy
and Often
the Least
Understood

After you finish reading this book and processing the insights provided, you'll think twice before equipping your sales force with more glossy brochures, updating your Web site with a new tagline, or plowing large volumes of cash into your next advertising or marketing initiative. Instead you'll probably think more about how to build and sustain a difference in the market by:

1. Determining the experience your customers want.

2. Finding the right people to deliver that experience.

3. Ensuring your people have the right operational processes to efficiently and effectively deliver experiences for your customers.

1.6 Your Brand Drives Your Work Culture

Professor Jim Doyle, who taught my MBA entrepreneurship class, defined culture in a way that I will never forget. I walked into his class thinking of work culture as something ubiquitous, intangible, and confusing. Jim said culture is, "the way we do things around here." What a truism this has become for me.

I have since learned that this quote about culture was first delivered by John Kotter in his masterful book on culture change, *Leading Change.* Work culture is nothing more than the way people do things (behaviors) inside a company. It's a very simple concept that is incredibly difficult to manage. Why? I'm glad you asked. Here's how it works:

Individuals have certain beliefs about the customers, partners, and their fellow employees in the companies they work for. These beliefs (whether correct or not) influence their attitudes, which directly impact the behaviors (actions) they exhibit from minute to minute, hour to hour, and day to day.

If a company wants to drive culture change, it must define the beliefs and behaviors employees should have and do. If employees don't have them, then leaders must be willing to invest the resources to find and develop employees who do (and transition out those who don't).

Truth
NUMBER

1

A Brand
Strategy Is
the Ultimate
Business
Strategy
and Often
the Least
Understood

> Truth #6: *Behaviors and Experiences Make the Invisible Visible* will provide insight into how to begin defining beliefs, behaviors, and experiences that will bring your brand strategy to life.

Let's review the logic here. If Company A has outlined the beliefs that are important to it with respect to delivering great customer service, then a set of behavioral norms that employees must be held accountable for can be documented. If Company A does not define the beliefs and behaviors yet leaders tell employees that they must deliver great customer service, then each employee will define how to do it in his or her own way, not the company's way.

An alternative is to write down what you believe about how to serve customers and the behaviors required to do it right. Then you can hold your people accountable for doing it exactly the way you want. If you simply say you want great customer service, your people will find hundreds of different ways they think will achieve it. You'll have no consistency. You won't achieve *Brand Integrity*.

Of course, this leads to utter chaos where all employees have the autonomy to define their own behavioral expectations. You'll be running an operation where everyone is doing his or her own thing. Think about your business. How far off am I from describing how you operate? Do you tell your employees how high quality your product is? Do they understand your beliefs about high quality?

Do you tell them that you strive to be the "employer of choice"? Do they understand what this means? What are your company's beliefs about why being an "employer of choice" is important? What behaviors do employees and other leaders all consistently exhibit to demonstrate this concept?

A brand strategy has the ability to drive your company culture. This is accomplished by clearly defining the brand concepts (values, principles, etc.) that define who your company is. For instance, the concepts below are meaningless (truly invisible) without behaviors to prove them.

- Excellent Customer Service
- Uncompromising Integrity
- Delivering High Quality
- Being the Employer of Choice

- Committed to Innovation
- Operational Efficiency
- Appreciating Diversity

Defining these types of concepts is a critical step in developing your company's brand strategy and defining your work culture.

> *Work culture can be defined as the way we do things around here.*

Before you know it, your brand strategy has not only defined your work culture, it has actually guided the transformation as employees' beliefs and behaviors become aligned, leading to a powerful force that impacts the way people think, speak, and behave in your company.

Companies that embrace this type of thinking are the true winners in their market. You know many of them by name because of the accomplishments they have made. What you may not know is all of the detail that has gone into defining the beliefs and behaviors

31

that drive their successful work cultures. Hats off to companies such as Outback Steakhouse, Dell Computer, Disney World, JetBlue Airlines, Southwest Airlines, Starbucks, The Westin, Ritz Carlton, and Enterprise Rent-a-Car. These companies appear to have figured out that:

- Their brand strategy is their business strategy.

- Their brand is about the experiences their people deliver, not just logos and taglines.

- The little things their people do consistently are much more important than the big things that they say.

- Their brand strategy is the single most important differentiator that makes them a great company and not just a good company.

Companies that define a strategy to drive their culture will win more, lose less, and make more money.

Truth
NUMBER

1

A Brand
Strategy Is
the Ultimate
Business
Strategy
and Often
the Least
Understood

1.7 The Ultimate Business Strategy Requires Top Business Objectives

A true measure of your company's brand strategy success: Are the leaders able to achieve the top business objectives?

One of the initial steps to getting started with creating a brand strategy is to develop those objectives. I'm not suggesting a lengthy list of goals you want your company to achieve. Rather, they should include no more than three to five key objectives to focus on along with action items, measures, timing, and employee ownership. Getting laser-focused on a few objectives will enable greater clarity and understanding among your employees as to what the most important initiatives are. Keeping them focused on fewer initiatives will lead to more success. The Ideas Into Action section below provides more detail about getting started with building your top business objectives.

BRAND CHALLENGE

"Our employee morale is a bit low and we sometimes lose good people."

DEVELOP TOP BUSINESS OBJECTIVES

If you don't know where you are going, how will you know when you get there?

Not having business objectives that you and your other leaders are on board with is like trying to sail around the world without a compass. You may be able to follow the sun and gain some perspective of your direction, but the chances of arriving at your desired destination are slim to none.

Bring a few leaders together to develop the top few most important business objectives. Working with this team, determine the most important areas of focus (goals, initiatives, measures) to achieve success.

Documenting your top business objectives will align your entire leadership team on what success looks like and will help generate the energy necessary to bring your brand strategy and vision to reality. Once you have documented the objectives, actions, and measures, you'll have a strong understanding of the conditions required for success with respect to your company's readiness (ability) and resources.

Don't fool yourself (or your team) into thinking you're ready to take on actions to hit objectives unless you're highly confident you can do so. In other words, don't set your people up for failure. Set them up for success. Hitting objectives takes tremendous energy and commitment. You and your team must be focused on doing the right things that will drive the sales and profitability of your company. Articulating your top business objectives will get you there!

Truth
NUMBER

1

A Brand Strategy Is the Ultimate Business Strategy and Often the Least Understood

SOLUTION

"Better align your people with your brand strategy and work will become more meaningful, accountability will increase, and employees will be more trusting of leadership. Your culture WILL improve."

Go to www.brandintegrity.com/truth1 to download a guide for creating top business objectives. This guide provides an exercise to get your leaders thinking about what the top objectives should be as well as an action planning template for documenting them and assigning accountability.

A Brand
Strategy Is
the Ultimate
Business
Strategy
and Often
the Least
Understood

Truth

1

A Brand
Strategy Is
the Ultimate
Business
Strategy
and Often
the Least
Understood

Truth
NUMBER

True Branding Is About Being Different, Not Saying Different Things

NUMBER

2

True Branding
Is About Being
Different,
Not Saying
Different
Things

TOPICS

2.1 The Essence of Differentiation: Sacrifice

2.2 Some Things Can Make You Different. Most Can't!

2.3 Change the Playing Field

IDEAS ····⟩ ACTION

1 Determine
Where Your
Company Is
on Its Path to
Achieving Brand
Integrity

2 Begin
Uncovering
Your Points
of Difference

2.1 The Essence of Differentiation: Sacrifice

We've all heard the saying, "you can't be all things to all people." Well, when building a compelling and sustainable brand strategy, it's true. A brand strategy requires the ingredient of differentiation. As a leader in your company, you must be creative with your team in the discovery and cultivation of differentiation.

Being different is difficult work. It requires incredible focus and discipline among leaders. You must focus on what truly makes your company easier to do business with and better than the competition. Once you get focused, don't lose it; the more out of focus your company becomes, the less different you will be. Customers and employees don't want sameness. Powerful differentiation is essential to being noticed, heard, and associated with something important.

2.2 Some Things Can Make You Different. Most Can't!

Almost every client that my firm has worked with believes they are different, yet most couldn't really articulate it in believable and measurable ways. In most cases, leaders in these organizations default to the two most referenced points of difference: service level and quality. They'd tell us, "We have the highest quality product," and "Our service is second to none." We asked, "Are you truly known for outstanding product quality?" or "Do you really deliver the best customer service in the market? What makes it different?"

These questions are typically followed by two reactions:

1. **The blank stare:** An uncomfortable moment where nothing is said. It may last only five seconds but it feels like an hour.

2. **Diarrhea of the mouth** (sorry for the horrific analogy, but if you've been through this as a consultant, you know how painful it can be): Incessant rambling about how great the quality and service are without really being able to express how they're any different from the competition. A completely ignorant and unrealistic expression of perceived differentiation that clearly does not exist.

"We have the best customer service."　　*"Okay, please provide it. Always!"*

Truth
NUMBER

2

True Branding
Is About Being
Different,
Not Saying
Different
Things

Interestingly, company leaders (and you know who you are) who think their company's point of difference consists of outstanding customer service and amazingly high-quality products and services end up doing the most whining because they don't feel they have a strong brand. Why is that? Because customers have come to expect those features and benefits. In most industries customer service and quality products/services have become price-to-entry[1] to compete with the most profitable and successful in the industry.

1 Price-to-entry: An attribute, association, and/or benefit your company delivers that is required to successfully compete in your industry. You have to have it!

The reality is that product quality and customer service have become an expectation and not a differentiator in a competitive market. That means your customers expect it. If you lower quality or service below what the customer is expecting, you will lose more often. You will not be able to change the customer's expectation and your competition will meet it. Or worse, exceed it.

However, there are many other ways to differentiate your organization and complement it with high quality and great service. The key is to discover what you want to be known for. Determine the attributes and associations that your company can own in the minds of the consumer, and complement it with consistently good or great quality and service.

"Consistency is king."

39

Seek to uncover a series of associations, personality characteristics, and attributes unique to your company. Then determine the level of service and quality needed to deliver your differentiation in ways that will enable you to kick your competition's ass and sustain your advantage over time.

Truth
NUMBER

2

True Branding
Is About Being
Different,
Not Saying
Different
Things

Starbucks doesn't *say* it's different, it *acts* different! Starbucks took a commodity product (i.e., coffee) and created a sustainable and competitive differentiation. The association it carved out was the Daytime Vacation Spot. A "third place" where you could go to lose yourself for a few minutes or a few hours each day. Starbucks does not advertise, promote, or even speak much about the quality of it coffee beans or the service level of baristas. It does, however, bring its differentiation to life through the design of stores and the employee and customer experiences in them.

You can bring leaders together and engage employees to deliver a differentiated experience. Doing so, and doing it consistently, will enable your company to achieve *Brand Integrity*.

2.3 Change the Playing Field

To truly differentiate in an industry of sameness, you will often need to change the rules of the game. Be bold. Uncover new ways to add value for customers. Try to do it in ways that also decrease your total cost of delivery. When successful, you'll have changed the playing field, bringing about a level of differentiation your company can be known for and profit from.

Cirque du Soleil changed the playing field in the circus industry. It has increased revenue by a factor of 22 percent over the last 10 years in an industry that has struggled to grow. Cirque du Soleil did not achieve its tremendous success by competing within the confines of the existing circus industry or by stealing customers from its main competitor, Ringling Brothers. Instead, it created uncontested market space that made the competition irrelevant. Cirque du Soleil established differentiation that did not exist in the market, and consumers wanted it.

BRAND CHALLENGE

"We want to be known for great customer service but are not seen as any different from our competition."

Cirque du Soleil did not sing the same song in a different key. I call what they did Rocking the Industry. They changed the playing field with very different circus experiences that were meaningful to the customers they were targeting.

Who else has rocked their industry?

JetBlue Airlines: Television at every seat. Leather seats with just a bit more room. The core of their brand: employees who appear to actually be happy and like their customers.

Jerry Jones (owner of the Dallas Cowboys): Corporate sponsorship and a training camp to create an event for fans.

Outback Steakhouse: No Rules, Just Right Policy and servers who sit down at your table.

Starbucks Coffee: Nomenclature to de-commoditize coffee (e.g., Tall, Grande, and Venti).

Howard Stern: Shock Jock content.

Apple: Style, ease of use, reliability, and design of products such as personal computers and iPods.

You may not be able to Rock Your Industry, but you can build differentiation into your company brand by leveraging creativity to establish truly memorable and meaningful experiences.

Believability is typically low when your company and employees only verbally promote and advertise differentiation. Most people won't believe it (and they shouldn't).

Uncovering uniqueness and differentiation is a must! If you choose not to, you'll find that the alternatives are not only less profitable, they're more costly. It costs more money to try to form desired perceptions in the minds of others when you sing the same song as everyone else. People get confused and over time they won't see your company and its offering as special or different in a meaningful way (and that's not good).

Truth
NUMBER

2

True Branding Is About Being Different, Not Saying Different Things

SOLUTION

"Personalize great customer service for your business by building proprietary work processes, employee behaviors, and customer experiences."

How do you ensure that you can differentiate in ways that are sustainable and profitable? Keep reading ...

Truth
NUMBER

2

True Branding
Is About Being
Different,
Not Saying
Different
Things

DETERMINE WHERE YOUR COMPANY IS ON ITS PATH TO ACHIEVING BRAND INTEGRITY

Begin to evaluate your company's current approach to thinking about and doing branding. Doing so is the first step to understanding your company's points of difference (or lack thereof). Take a look at the way your company communicates its brand to employees and customers. By doing so, you'll gain an appreciation for the current philosophy/approach your employees are using that will hinder or strengthen your brand.

Below are three types of branding for you and your leadership team to consider. Each of them is required to achieve *Brand Integrity* and differentiate your company. Along with each type of branding, I've provided a sample set of tactics. Review them and identify which ones you have been committing resources to up until this point in your company's development.

1. **Communications Branding:** Pushing glossy paper and pretty pictures that make you look good to those who might be willing to read it. Some examples include:

   • Advertising

   • Coupons and special promotions

   • Web site

   • Direct mail

   • Public relations

   • Event sponsorships

2. **Customer Experience Branding:** Uncovering the areas where your brand interacts with customers and can have an impact on their perceptions. Below are some examples:

- Humorous or highly engaging advertising

- Highly interactive Web site

- Predefined customer service guidelines

- Engaging trade show participation

- Collection and use of customer satisfaction feedback

- Consistent process for thanking customers

3. **Culture Branding:** Documenting the behaviors and work processes necessary for your company to truly do what you say it will do and to hold employees accountable for doing it. Some of the steps include:

- Including brand expectations in job descriptions

- Hiring employees using the brand as a guide

- Training leaders to be brand ambassadors

- Orienting employees on how to deliver the brand in their day-to-day jobs

- Conducting quarterly brand-behavior assessments for all employees

- Holding annual performance evaluations that include brand-behavior assessment

> Truth #8: *Gaining Buy-in Is the Only Way to Execute a Brand Strategy* will take you into much greater detail about how to develop an employee performance program that drives Culture Branding.

Truth
NUMBER

2

True Branding
Is About Being
Different,
Not Saying
Different
Things

Truth
NUMBER

2

True Branding
Is About Being
Different,
Not Saying
Different
Things

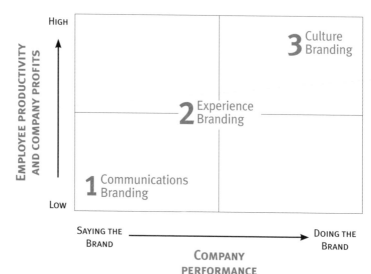

If your company's primary branding efforts are on the Communications Branding level, you can't possibly be consistently delivering experiences that engage employees and motivate them to provide meaningful experiences to customers — experiences that customers will be willing to pay a premium for because they differentiate your offering in a way that makes their life better. Unless your focus is on developing and managing a work culture that holds employees accountable for doing the brand, you won't be able to enhance employee productivity and drive greater profits for your company using your brand as your primary vehicle.

If, however, your company is focusing on Culture Branding, the customer experience and communications branding become much more powerful with respect to driving customer loyalty and sales. Simply because your employees are more prepared to *be* and *do* the brand.

To determine where your company falls on the Path to Achieving Brand Integrity, go to www.brandintegrity.com/truth2 and download and complete the exercise provided. Then consider where your greatest opportunities are to enhance your company's brand and point of difference.

Truth
NUMBER

2

True Branding
Is About Being
Different,
Not Saying
Different
Things

BEGIN UNCOVERING YOUR POINTS OF DIFFERENCE

What makes your company different? To find out, ask yourself some insightful questions.

To get started on the pathway of determining your company's true points of difference, you'll need to:

1. Determine your **strengths** and **meaningful benefits** in the minds of your customers. Ask:

   • What are three main reasons you like to do business with our company?

   • What is the one thing we do that our competition doesn't?

   • If our company closed its doors tomorrow, what would you miss most one week from now? Six months? Twelve months from now?

For a complete list of Point of Difference questions, go to www.brandintegrity.com/truth2.

2. Document the **reasons to believe** that prove your strengths and meaningful benefits. These are credibility proof points that instill understanding and confidence that your company's product or service will meet or exceed customer expectations. Turn the page for five ways to increase the reasons to believe in the minds of your employees and customers.

Truth

NUMBER

2

True Branding
Is About Being
Different,
Not Saying
Different
Things

Use 5-year-old logic: Speak to customers in such a way that a 5-year-old could understand the benefits. Share the basic facts that can be easily understood and quickly related to. For example, PAETEC Communications, a leading telecommunications provider, makes a claim that all calls to their service center are answered 94 percent of the time with a live voice within 20 seconds. This claim is simple, straightforward, and (to those needing service) very beneficial.

Give value first through a personal experience: Figure out ways to offer customers a sample of your product or service and have an experience before purchasing. Product and service sampling and/or a demonstration can prove to be a great way to build reasons to believe. Let them try before they buy!

Brag about your heritage: Detail the pedigree behind your product or service. Include your company history, processes, or unique brand names. Make sure they're really meaningful. But if your customers will think, "Who cares?" then stay away from heritage.

Sharing testimonials from customers, experts in the field, or the media: Use both written and video testimonials. If economically viable, go for video testimonials whenever possible. Your customers will almost always believe other customers way more than you and your employees.

Risk a guarantee: The power of your guarantee is directly linked to the level of risk you and your company are perceived to take. To be effective, the guarantee must maximize customer confidence rather than reduce legal risk. At Brand Integrity Inc., we offer a 100 percent guarantee on all projects, stating in our contract that we will deliver everything stated in our contract at the agreed-upon investment or work for no fee until we do. Simple, straightforward, and it takes away some of the perceived risk.

Pick two or three of these reasons to believe and challenge your team to come up with ways to deliver them.

So, branding is about managing perceptions and uncovering and delivering a difference in the market. How will you ensure that you can do this in ways that are sustainable and profitable?

Keep reading …

Truth
NUMBER

2

True Branding
Is About Being
Different,
Not Saying
Different
Things

Truth
NUMBER

If You Think You Know Your Brand Image, You're Probably Wrong

Truth
NUMBER

3

If You Think
You Know Your
Brand Image,
You're Probably
Wrong

TOPICS

3.1 Knowing What Customers Think

3.2 People Define Your Brand Image — With or Without You

3.3 Customers Don't Know What They Don't Know

3.4 Customers Have a Job to Do

3.5 The Target Audience Universe

IDEAS ····> ACTION

1 Conduct Brand Image Assessments

2 Determine Your Customers' Desired Outcomes

49

3.1 Knowing What Customers Think

Do you believe you really know what your customers think of your company, products, and services? How sure are you? When was the last time you asked them? Time and again, I work with leaders in companies who believe they know what their customers think, and most of the time they're wrong! This information is critical to being able to sell more stuff. Understanding what customers think enables you to successfully position your products and services to best meet the needs and desires of those who are willing to pay for them.

When customers think of your company, who or what do they associate you with? Which attributes influence their purchase decision? Do they understand the benefits that your company delivers? Do they believe you're different from your competition? And most important, do customers understand what they are trying to have satisfied by your company and its offerings? They may think they know. But are they right?

This is a lot to think about, I know. But you can get tangled up in your underwear and confuse the heck out of every employee in your company if you don't think this through clearly. You can also confuse your customers — a surefire way to get them to start thinking about your competition. If customers aren't satisfied by what you provide, they'll go elsewhere regardless of whether they'll actually get what they want.

WHAT? WAIT A MINUTE. WHY WILL THEY GO TO MY COMPETITION?

The purpose of a brand strategy is to influence what people think about your company. Whether those people are employees, customers, partners, vendors, or shareholders doesn't matter. They all have two things in common:

1. They all have perceptions about your brand (your company).

2. They all have desired outcomes they want to achieve. They may not know them, but they do have them. If you can't satisfy them, they'll look elsewhere for a company that can!

Truth
NUMBER

3

If You Think
You Know Your
Brand Image,
You're Probably
Wrong

50

3.2 People Define Your Brand Image — With or Without You

If you go looking for your brand image, the only place you'll find it is in the minds of customers. If you don't define your brand, they will do it for you.

The brand image of your company is in the minds of the people you do business with. Not just your customers and employees, but also your partners and vendors. The perceptions they hold to be true dramatically impact how much and how often they will do business with you. These perceptions drive their actions. In the case of customers, the actions come in the form of increased loyalty, which leads to increased sales. For employees, perceptions also drive loyalty, which has a direct impact on work effort, productivity, and your company's culture.

Truth
NUMBER

3

If You Think
You Know Your
Brand Image,
You're Probably
Wrong

The branding process begins by understanding your target audience (customers, employees, and other stakeholders) and determining what they want to receive from their relationship with your brand. Then your company can structure its brand to best meet those customers where they are and take them to where they want to be.

There are four primary areas of your brand that influence what your employees and customers think of your company. Knowing these areas dramatically increases the likelihood that you can implement a brand strategy that will enable customers to buy more stuff, more often.

1. **Attributes and associations:** An identity or set of themes based on descriptions used to describe your company, its people, and its products and services. This part of the brand highlights personality characteristics that can represent a relationship a customer has with your brand. Like a person, your brand has a personality that provides depth of feelings to the relationship with stakeholders.

2. **Competitive strengths:** A perspective on meaningful benefits delivered to customers as well as points of difference and points of parity when compared to competitive offerings.

51

3. **Concerns and weaknesses:** A realistic view of concerns that affect product and/or service delivery, employee morale and productivity, customer loyalty, and sales.

4. **Work culture:** A perspective on what it's like to work for your company based on the way employees operate and the work processes and employee behaviors that enable customer experiences.

Truth
NUMBER

3

If You Think
You Know Your
Brand Image,
You're Probably
Wrong

How do you discover the brand image of your company? Simple. Ask.

Ask customers what words come to mind when they think of your company. Ask them for the top three reasons they like to do business with your company. Ask them what they would miss most if your company closed its doors tomorrow. Find out what some of their concerns are in regard to doing business with your company and using your products or services.

Gather these insights and you should begin to get a clear picture of your company's current brand image. Remember, it's what's in *their* minds that counts, not yours. What they say goes! They, the customers, are the holders of your brand image.

Keep in mind, though, that customers don't always know what they don't know.

3.3 Customers Don't Know What They Don't Know

Determining your existing brand image is only half the battle. Once you know, then you need to understand why it is what it is. You need to figure out why customers think of you as slow, when you thought they would think of you as fast. Is it the way your company's products work? Is it the way employees deliver service? Or is it because of the expectations customers have of themselves, coupled with their expectations of how your company can help them? The answer to each of these questions is, yes! It's typically all of these things.

BRAND CHALLENGE

*"I think I know
what our
customers want."*

The problem is, sometimes customers don't know what they don't know. And you need to help them figure it out.

Henry Ford revolutionized the automobile with little insight from customers. You may be familiar with Mr. Ford's famous quote, "You can have any color you want as long as it's black." Well, a not-so-famous quote tells an even greater story. It has been reported that when asked why he didn't seek more input from potential customers when devising the first automobile, Henry Ford said, "If I asked customers what they wanted, they would have told me faster horses." The moral of the story is that sometimes your customers do not know what they do not know. Therefore, it's your responsibility to help them figure it out.

Truth
NUMBER

3

If You Think
You Know Your
Brand Image,
You're Probably
Wrong

You can do this by helping customers to more clearly understand the jobs they are trying to get done.

JOBS! WHAT IS HE TALKING ABOUT NOW?

3.4 Customers Have a Job to Do

Yes, customers will form an impression of your company and products based on their experience. But before they even try you out, they'll form impressions based on what they think they are trying to accomplish by doing business with you. In some cases, they may not even know what they're looking for. This is where you come in.

All customers have a *job* to do — something they are trying to accomplish by using your product or service. Starbucks figured out that customers had a job to do and it wasn't just to buy coffee. Starbucks figured out that customers wanted a "third place" to spend their time between work or school and home. The customers' job was to find a place where they could briefly escape — for three minutes or 30. Since Starbucks uncovered this job, it was able to build a brand strategy to cater to it. In other words, the job — not the coffee product — became the unit of analysis for Starbucks as it helped customers understand their business, its offerings, and how to enjoy them.

SOLUTION

"You could be wrong. Why take the chance? Ask them and then you'll know for sure. They'll love you for asking."

Truth
NUMBER

3

If You Think
You Know Your
Brand Image,
You're Probably
Wrong

What jobs do your customers want to do? What do they need to get done today that your product or service could help them accomplish? Once you understand the jobs your customers are trying to get done, then you can focus on the outcomes they want to achieve. Starbucks realized customers desired greater social interaction, a more comfortable and eclectic seating environment, friendlier and more knowledgeable staff, and greater education on unique coffee and coffee-related drinks. So the company built its strategy in ways that enable customers to *hire* Starbucks to help them achieve those desired outcomes.

Don't start building your strategy by analyzing customer demographic and psychographic characteristics. Begin by uncovering the jobs they want to accomplish. Doing so will spark the creative energy and results required to build a differentiated brand image in the market.

Once you understand the jobs, you can focus on the desired outcomes for those jobs. The outcomes become a customer wish list for what they need and want in a relationship with your company, products, and services and each job will have its own wish list.

The best ways to identify those jobs and desired outcomes is to ask and observe.

DESIRED OUTCOME METHODOLOGY

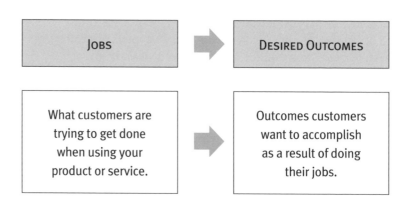

JOBS		DESIRED OUTCOMES
What customers are trying to get done when using your product or service.		Outcomes customers want to accomplish as a result of doing their jobs.

When the founder of Sony, Akio Morita, led his organization on the development of the Walkman, he did not have them engage in typical marketing research. Instead, efforts were made to better understand what people were trying to get done in their lives, and then figuring out how Sony's electronics could help them to do those things better. The Walkman was born. Sony could have studied the market to see how many cassette tape players were being sold and to whom. But that might have led to Sony misjudging the target consumer as well as the size of the market.

When asking customers about jobs and desired outcomes, be careful not to accept their first answers. Don't ask what they want; ask them what they *need*. Then continue to follow up with questions as to why they think they need it. A series of "why" questions can take you beyond the initially stated solutions to the real desired outcomes.

Truth
NUMBER

3

If You Think
You Know Your
Brand Image,
You're Probably
Wrong

If this approach doesn't seem entirely customer-driven, keep in mind that customers aren't always experts in your product or service category. Often they don't know what they don't know. Henry Ford thought customers would have asked for faster horses. What do you think Steve Jobs' customers wanted before Apple developed the concept for the iPod? Who would have thought they wanted to identify with being cool while importing their entire music library onto a device smaller than a credit card? Probably not Steve Jobs, nor the customers themselves. The customers' job was to organize all of their music in one spot. One of the desired outcomes was to look cool and trendy. Apple's product design and marketing execution are focused on helping customers do both.

3.5 The Target Audience Universe

By now you should be in complete agreement with me that it's critical to know the brand image held by your most important customers. Take a moment to ponder the following: Who are your most important customers? Which ones are your company's primary customers? What makes them so important? Is it quantity of product or service purchased, profitability per sale, long-term growth opportunity, or short-term revenue? You need to know the answers to these types of questions if you want to build the most accurate image for your brand. You'll find that you not only need to focus on the customers who purchase, but also on the various other audiences that play a role in the purchase process. Your target audience will typically consist of at least two or more of the following:

Truth
NUMBER

3

If You Think
You Know Your
Brand Image,
You're Probably
Wrong

1. **Segments that you target:** Large groups of consumers whose purchases you believe are most important for you to reach your growth objectives.

2. **Buyers who can hire and fire you:** Individuals who actually make the purchase decision regarding your offering.

3. **End-users of your offering:** These are the people who have a job to do and desired outcomes to achieve.

4. **Influencers who help you:** These people have some knowledge about your offering and/or knowledge about the jobs and desired outcomes of the end-users. They can help you to communicate the benefits of your offering.

5. **Gatekeepers who let you in:** These are the people who play a lesser role in the purchase decision, but can be an initial hurdle to gaining the attention of the influencers and buyers.

For some of your company's products and services, only a few of the target audiences need to be taken into consideration as you begin to understand your brand image and how to influence it. In some cases, your brand image is critical across all of them.

Make no mistake about it — you must begin the process by first thinking through the target audience universe so that you know whose perceptions are most important in trying to sell more of your stuff. Next you need to reach out to the folks and ask questions to gain understanding and appreciation for their current perceptions — the brand image they have of your company and its offering. You can then begin to discover the jobs your most important customers are trying to get done and the outcomes they want to achieve.

CONDUCT BRAND IMAGE ASSESSMENTS

No more leaving your brand image unknown. Or worse yet, simply sitting by and allowing employees and customers to define it without you. Be proactive. Ask employees and customers what they think of your company and its products and services. There are at least two brand image assessments for you to conduct:

1. Employee Brand Image Assessment:

This serves the purpose of understanding your company's current brand image in your employees' minds. Gaining their perspectives will provide you with initial insights on their beliefs and behaviors that are influencing your work culture and the customer experience. This assessment MUST be completely confidential in order to be valid. The sample size to use depends on the size of your company. For a company with 100 employees, I would recommend a sample of 30 employees. For a company with 1,000 employees, I would recommend a sample of 100 employees. When in doubt, I recommend going smaller on the sample size as you can always conduct more assessments. This assessment should be done using the Internet when possible. At Brand Integrity Inc., we built our own survey tool that is not sold to the public. However, I have heard that www.surveymonkey.com is a good way to go. There are lots of others.

2. Customer Brand Image Assessment:

This will enable you to better understand the brand image (perceptions) customers have that influence their ongoing loyalty and purchase habits of your product or service. It's most efficient and useful when done through telephone-based interviews. Of course, most insightful (but also more costly) are face-to-face interviews with a skilled interviewer. The Web-based assessment can be used, but it has proven to be less effective because of the limited ability to probe into the insights that are truly driving customer behaviors.

Truth
NUMBER

3

If You Think You Know Your Brand Image, You're Probably Wrong

For both the employee and customer brand image assessments, you will want to focus on four primary areas. Each of these areas is listed below with a few sample questions that have proven to be quite effective. A gap analysis between employee groups and employees and customers will be of great value to you and your leadership. To ensure a sound gap analysis, you need to ask similar, if not identical, questions of the various groups.

Truth
NUMBER

3

If You Think
You Know Your
Brand Image,
You're Probably
Wrong

- **Attributes and associations:** Questions to stimulate descriptions of your company's brand identity.

  - When you think of _____ Company, what's the first word that comes to mind?

  - If you were to describe _____ Company to someone who doesn't know anything about it, what would you say?

- **Competitive strengths:** Questions to gain perspective on meaningful benefits delivered to customers and points of difference and points of parity when compared to competitive offerings.

  - What are the three main reasons why customers like to do business at/with _____ Company?

  - If _____ Company ceased to exist, what would customers miss most?

  - What does _____ Company do that others in the industry would never do?

- **Concerns and weaknesses:** A realistic view of concerns that impact product and/or service delivery, employee morale and productivity, customer loyalty, and new sales.

  - What are the three most frequent complaints you hear about _____ Company from customers?

  - What are the three most frequent complaints you hear about _____ Company from employees? (Please capture your thoughts regardless of whether or not they are positive.)

- **Work Culture:** Questions that lead to a perspective on what it's like to work for the company based on the behaviors employees demonstrate and the performance standards they are held accountable for. From the customers' view, these questions are more focused on the experience of doing business with your company as a result of employee behaviors and operational processes.

Truth
NUMBER

3

If You Think
You Know Your
Brand Image,
You're Probably
Wrong

- If you were to describe _____ Company as an animal, what animal would you choose and why?

- What behaviors does a _____ Company employee consistently demonstrate for customers that are admired and lead to loyalty and referrals?

- On a scale of one to ten, where one is very poor and ten is outstanding, how would you rate _____ Company as a place to work? Why?

 A very detailed guide with many more questions to choose from, along with types of responses to look for when analyzing the results, can be found by visiting www.brandintegrity.com/truth3.

DETERMINE YOUR CUSTOMERS' DESIRED OUTCOMES

After completing the customer brand image assessment work, you can begin to build a framework for better understanding your most important customers. The goal is to document the desired outcomes that each customer group wants to achieve when doing business with your company.

The following Brand Integrity Desired Outcome Methodology can be used to build the framework for customers. I am assuming as you begin to use this framework that you have a grasp of which customer segments are the most important to the future growth of your company. If you don't, then think that piece through before getting started with this method.

The methodology begins with documenting themes that capture the high-level things a customer segment values in a working relationship with your people, products, and/or service. After conducting a brand image assessment and asking questions about perceived benefits and points of difference, you should be able to capture a few high-level themes. To assist you with getting to the themes, ask yourself the reasons a customer does business with your company. If you are a hotel, ask yourself why people stay in a hotel. List as many reasons as you can. From that list, you will be able to combine similar ideas and develop four to six themes.

Truth
NUMBER

3

If You Think
You Know Your
Brand Image,
You're Probably
Wrong

Next, for each theme, determine the jobs your customers are trying to get done by using your product or service. For each theme, draft two or three jobs that you think customers want to achieve.

Finally, it's time to draft the desired outcomes. You can get to the desired outcomes fastest by playing the Why? game. Keep asking why questions behind each job or stated need or want. Continuing to ask why will lead you to the deeper meaning behind the outcome.

Below is an example of the Brand Integrity Desired Outcome Methodology being used for an independent senior living community.

Theme: Wellness *(A major reason seniors move into senior living communities is that they want to maintain or increase their overall wellness.)*

Job: Improving access to health care. *(This is what seniors are trying to get done. The job they are trying to accomplish.)*

Desired Outcomes: *(What seniors are trying to achieve when they perform a job.)*

1. Know medical care is readily available when needed (get in to a doctor without waiting for an appointment).

2. Increase the likelihood they will live a longer, healthier life.

The next piece of the methodology includes the obstacles that individuals face. Sticking with the independent senior living community example, an obstacle would be the roadblocks that get in the way of accomplishing a job. For instance, if the job is to improve access to health care, then an obstacle might be the vast quantity of diverse viewpoints that are communicated in the marketplace. The overabundance of information may be confusing, making such a situation a true obstacle to getting better access to health care.

Truth
NUMBER

3

If You Think
You Know Your
Brand Image,
You're Probably
Wrong

The next step is gaining customers' perspective so that you can understand your greatest opportunity to be different when compared to your competition. Once desired outcomes are documented based on your leadership team's perspective, you must take the work to your customers and have them rank the priority of the desired outcomes. There are two perspectives you will want them to rank:

1. How important the desired outcome is to them.

2. How satisfied they are with their current ability to achieve the desired outcome.

Have customers rank each desired outcome once for importance and once for satisfaction using a scale of one to five, with five being most important and most satisfied and one being not at all important and not at all satisfied. Desired outcomes that are ranked high in importance and low in satisfaction should become areas of focus for you and your team as you build your brand strategy. The Point of Difference Opportunity Grid on page 63 provides a strategic way of thinking about desired outcomes as they pertain to your ability to differentiate your brand. This information will be critical to your success in building the brand strategy that is covered in Truth #6.

Use the following formula to calculate the Point of Difference Opportunity Score:

Point of Difference = Importance Score + (Importance Score – Satisfaction Score)

The reason the point of difference is calculated as a function of importance is because in the brand-building arena where experiences can be developed to delight customers, those experiences can also change the level of importance of a particular offering. Therefore, as part of the brand strategy development process, leaders should have a focus on trying to uncover desired outcomes that are ranked as low importance but could become much more important by delivering the right experience.

Truth
NUMBER
3

If You Think
You Know Your
Brand Image,
You're Probably
Wrong

Below are descriptions of the four quadrants used to organize the Point of Difference Opportunity.

Quadrant 1
Opportunity to Disinvest: In this case, satisfaction is high and importance is low. Typically not a great place to invest your resources unless this is a cash cow and your company is a leading provider.

Quadrant 2
Competitive Opportunity: With importance and satisfaction both scoring on the high end, you can expect lots of competition to be focusing on these desired outcomes. You probably need to compete here in order to be well-positioned in your market.

Quadrant 3
Point of Difference Opportunity: This is the area that you've discovered is high in importance, but customers are not satisfied. Helping customers to achieve desired outcomes here could provide a sound competitive advantage and a real differentiator for your product or service.

Quadrant 4
Importance Opportunity: This is the most overlooked quadrant which can have the biggest impact on solidifying your company's point of difference in the market. It is in this quadrant that you can home in on the desired outcomes that customers ranked as low importance and low satisfaction and find ways to increase the importance of them. Importance can be increased by delivering an experience that makes an outcome more meaningful. If they have an experience with your product or service and achieve a desired outcome, the relative strength of the experience can single-handedly increase their perceived importance for that outcome.

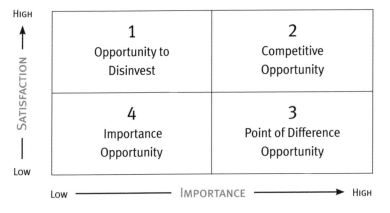

HIGH	**1** Opportunity to Disinvest	**2** Competitive Opportunity
LOW	**4** Importance Opportunity	**3** Point of Difference Opportunity

SATISFACTION

LOW ——————— IMPORTANCE ——————→ HIGH

POINT OF DIFFERENCE OPPORTUNITY GRID

In summary, the Brand Integrity Desired Outcome Methodology will position you and your team to achieve the following:

1. Determine and prioritize what your primary customers want in a relationship with your company.

2. Understand how customers measure the value of their desired outcomes.

3. Appreciate the obstacles that prohibit them from achieving their desired outcomes.

4. Understand the greatest areas for your company to be different based on your ability to help customers reach under-satisfied and important desired outcomes.

Go to www.brandintegrity.com/truth3. There you will find a template that can be used to organize and prioritize your customers' desired outcomes.

63

Truth
NUMBER

Only Wimps and Egomaniacs Are Afraid to Investigate Their Company's Reality

Truth
NUMBER

Only
Wimps and
Egomaniacs
Are Afraid to
Investigate
Their
Company's
Reality

Topics

4.1 Reality. Who Owns It?

4.2 Ask and You Will Receive

4.3 Show Some Guts! Investigate the Seven Realities

Ideas ····⟩ Action

1 Investigate
  Your Business
  Reality

4.1 Reality. Who Owns It?

Have you ever heard the term "spinning your reality"? Spinning reality is in reference to forming your own opinion of a situation based on the input processed in your mind. We all do it. It's how we form perceptions of situations that drive our decision-making, or lack of decision-making.

Truth
NUMBER
4
Only Wimps and Egomaniacs Are Afraid to Investigate Their Company's Reality

You can assume that every leader and employee in your company holds their own truths about reality. Each person takes in the information, processes it, and forms their own beliefs that ultimately influence their attitudes and drive their behaviors.

In other words, each employee and leader in your company owns their own reality. The more stubborn, ignorant, or egotistical they are, the more difficult it will be to shift their realities.

To build a brand strategy that will cultivate and enhance your work culture, your leadership team has to investigate the reality as seen through the eyes of leaders and employees.

4.2 Ask and You Will Receive

How will you get the information you need from your team to really understand their realities? I am glad you asked. Your question is very simple and requires a very complex answer.

Here's the answer. You ASK them! But, you must ask them the right questions in the right manner. See, I told you this would get complex.

In all seriousness, it is that simple. You just need to ask the right questions (direct, strategic, and important) in the right environment (safe and confidential).

Holding meaningful conversations with leaders and employees and asking the right questions will enable your people to say the things that just can't be said. You know, the kind of statements and ideas that employees will hold to themselves to keep under the radar or to protect their butts from office politics that might hinder their job/career growth.

Truth
NUMBER

4

Only
Wimps and
Egomaniacs
Are Afraid to
Investigate
Their
Company's
Reality

"Please be candid with your
opinions about what it's like
to work here."

"Does she really want
to know what I think?
Can I trust her?"

If you don't ask, you definitely won't receive.

Wimps and egomaniacs don't like to investigate the realities of their top lieutenants and employees. You know these leaders. These wimps are afraid of what they might hear so it's easier for them to not ask and to press on, often swimming upstream to get anything accomplished on time and within budget. These wimps typically don't mind getting their ass kicked by the competition as long as they stay in the game. The egomaniacs believe they already know what others are thinking and feel pretty confident that they can generate enough of the insights and ideas to keep the company competitive and on course.

Are you one of these types of leaders? Are you comfortable being the kind of leader who has employees and other leaders blowing smoke up your ass, telling you what they think you want to hear while withholding valuable insights and ideas for fear of negative repercussions? Are you willing to wimp out and move forward without the answers you need? Are you an egomaniac with all the answers you need? If you can answer yes to these questions, then I recommend skipping to the next chapter.

If, however, you can get comfortable with the assumption that you have a better chance of uncovering the truths about your business if more people have a say, then stick with me as I explain how to go about investigating your own reality.

Truth
NUMBER

4

Only
Wimps and
Egomaniacs
Are Afraid to
Investigate
Their
Company's
Reality

Let's face it. Virtually all leaders on your team and many of your employees think they have a better way for your company to do something. And you know what? Many of them are right. However, none of them knows more than the sum of everyone's ideas. Can you buy into this? It's rare that any one person really knows more than the collective wisdom of a group of individuals.

Someone really smart once said, "No one is as smart as all of us." I have no idea who said it, but I believe he/she would really appreciate the truth of this chapter.

Powerful thinking occurs when you have the opportunity to explore various viewpoints.

4.3 Show Some Guts! Investigate the Seven Realities

Don't be a wimp! Get ready to challenge closely held assumptions about what's really going on in your company. Prepare yourself to learn, in great detail, the current state of your people's beliefs, which will enable you to make smarter decisions to improve for the future.

To conduct a proper investigation, schedule conversations between people in your company and a trained interviewer. These will be one-on-one discussions held in a confidential environment. I strongly recommend you hire an outside interviewer in order to ensure greater confidence in the confidential nature of the process. When your people know for sure their thoughts will be held strictly confidential, they will reveal a more accurate picture of what's going on with your company. In addition, hidden agendas will be more easily exposed and shared, which can lead to more efficient brand-building efforts.

From a brand-building perspective, there are typically seven different realities for you to investigate.

1. ACHIEVING DESIRED BUSINESS RESULTS

Quite simply, this is the "how are we doing" reality. Remember, people's perceptions are very powerful. You need to find out what they really think about the business results of your company's efforts with respect to the viewpoints of other employees as well as customers. A couple of good questions to ask leaders include:

- How well do operational and financial results reflect high performance of our company in comparison to our best competitors?

- How well have goals concerning employee motivation and satisfaction been achieved?

2. DRIVING DESIRED CULTURE

Does your leadership have the focus and alignment to drive desired behaviors that inspire and motivate employees to deliver exceptional service for customers? Answers to some insightful questions on the topic of organizational culture (the way we work around here) will provide you facts about the current behaviors that have become norms inside your company. Good or bad, these behaviors must be exposed and effectively managed as part of the brand-building process. A few good questions to ask leaders include:

- How well do we provide the leadership and customer focus needed for our company to achieve world-class performance?

- How well do our employees understand our goals and objectives?

- How well do our human resource (talent management) processes enable our company to recruit, hire, train, and develop high-performing individuals?

Truth
NUMBER

Only
Wimps and
Egomaniacs
Are Afraid to
Investigate
Their
Company's
Reality

3. Knowing Your Target Customers

How well do your people know the customers they serve? They may know more than you think, and could be holding on to valuable insights that could help you sell more stuff to more people. Or worse, they might not know as much as you think, leading to a diminished overall experience for the end customers. Uncover their knowledge of customer segments, actual purchasers, and the purchase influencers. A few good questions to ask leaders include:

Truth
NUMBER

4

Only
Wimps and
Egomaniacs
Are Afraid to
Investigate
Their
Company's
Reality

- How well do we understand our customers and their wants, needs, and challenges?

- How well do we manage customer relationships to enhance satisfaction, loyalty, and referrals?

- How well do we capture customer satisfaction data and utilize the information for improvement?

- How well do we understand our customers' decision-making process? Do we know how to reach the decision-makers?

- How well do we know which customers are most valuable today and in the future?

4. Understanding Experiences

Two types of experiences must be uncovered to truly understand the reality your company is delivering: the employee experience and the customer experience. Employee experiences are the things your company is doing to make work a rewarding and enjoyable place for employees.

Customer experiences are those interactions customers have with your people, products, and services that drive loyalty, referrals, and increased sales. Understanding how well your people know the customer experiences that are delivered is critical to beginning the development of a brand strategy. You might be shocked at the various awareness levels among your team regarding the experiences that are delighting or frustrating your customers. A few good questions to ask leaders include:

- How well do we understand the experiences that employees and customers have with our company?

- How well do we manage the customer relationship to generate greater loyalty and referrals?

- How well do employees articulate what it is that makes our company special (different or unique) in the marketplace?

5. Recognizing Your Company's Brand Positioning

Does your company have strategic, well-defined positioning in the marketplace? How well do leaders and employees throughout your company truly understand your unique positioning when compared to competitive offerings? How well does the marketplace (your target customers) know "who you are" as a company?

Truth
NUMBER

4

Only Wimps and Egomaniacs Are Afraid to Investigate Their Company's Reality

Positioning is about owning a place in the mind of your target customers. Unless your leaders and employees understand the positioning your company is vying for, it is very difficult for them to understand the relevance of their actions to strengthening that positioning. Uncovering employee perceptions about your unique (or not unique) positioning is critical to knowing how aligned your people are with your strategy. A few good questions to ask leaders include:

- How well do we positively shape or influence what customers think of our company?

- How well have we positively shaped or influenced what employees think of our company?

- How well do we understand what drives brand preference and loyalty within our primary target markets?

6. Implementing Important Initiatives

Many companies do a great job creating strategic initiatives only to fail time and again when it comes to implementing them. Asking leaders for their thoughts about how well your company develops action plans and assigns responsibilities and ownership will provide you great insight into their confidence level and frustrations when it comes to implementation.

Even greater insights can be gathered when you find out their thoughts about accountability. If your company is one where ownership is typically assigned and people feel accountable for results, then you will appreciate knowing why this culture is favorable for your people. If, however, accountability is relatively unheard of in your company, then understanding your leaders' thoughts about why this is a problem and how it can be solved will provide great insights that will enable you to implement more effectively.

At the end of the day, every company wants to do a great job implementing strategic initiatives. The reality is, most companies really stink at it. Have some guts — find out where you and your leadership team stand. A few good questions to ask leaders include:

- How well do we establish goals and objectives with reasonable timelines for achieving them?

- How well do we devise action plans, set timelines and accountability, and stick to them in order to achieve our goals?

- How well do we communicate strategic initiatives, establish ownership to drive success, and hold people accountable for implementation results?

7. Marketing Effectively to Customers

Are your marketing efforts responsible in the minds of your own people? Does the leadership feel confident knowing who the most important customers are to target with your offering? If so, do they know how to best communicate with them by effectively allocating resources to your marketing and communication efforts? You want your leadership to be proud of the marketing activities that are driving customer acquisition and loyalty.

The best way to find out how proud or disenfranchised leaders are is to determine their current perceptions. Your leaders are the brand ambassadors for your product or service. You need to be certain you know their perceptions about effective ways to market to customers. Even your least savvy marketers may surprise you with great insights on how to more effectively connect with your most important customers. A few good questions to ask leaders include:

- How well do we know where and to whom customers go when gathering information about our products and services? How well do we know which of these sources carries the most weight with them?

- How well do our current marketing activities drive or support customer acquisition, retention, and referrals?

- How do our current marketing materials (brochures, Web site, advertising, etc.) assist us with getting more customers?

- How well do our current marketing activities/materials deliver a concise and accurate portrayal of "who we are" as an organization and/or a product or service?

IDEAS ·····⟩ ACTION

INVESTIGATE YOUR BUSINESS REALITY

Force yourself and others that lead your company to investigate the reality of your business. Don't be a chicken. Too many leaders are afraid to ask the questions necessary to find out how the company and its leaders are really doing. They are afraid to challenge their own assumptions. They fear being wrong.

Using the questions listed in the previous pages as your starting point, you can investigate your company's reality in the minds of your leaders. Once you have their perspective, administer the same set of questions to gain feedback from employees.

When asking these "how are we doing" questions you will want respondents to answer in two different ways: with emotion and with logic. First, have them rank their response on a scale of one to seven to elicit an emotional response.

Here is a recommended ranking scale:

1 = Exceptional   5 = Inadequate
2 = Very Good   6 = Poor
3 = Good   7 = None
4 = Adequate

Truth
NUMBER

4

Only
Wimps and
Egomaniacs
Are Afraid to
Investigate
Their
Company's
Reality

Next, have the interviewer ask for the why behind the ranking. Having the respondent explain why will force them to explain the logic behind their thinking.

For a more complete set of interview questions and a more detailed approach for conducting the Investigating Reality Interview, go to www.brandintegrity.com/truth4.

Truth

NUMBER

4

Only
Wimps and
Egomaniacs
Are Afraid to
Investigate
Their
Company's
Reality

Truth
NUMBER

Marketing and Advertising Can Kill Your Brand

. . . .

TOPICS

Could you have imagined 10 years ago that you'd be able to type a keyword into your computer and instantly access a global database of knowledge? Who could have imagined that a company like Google would become such a pervasive part of our lives that now nearly everyone we know "googles"? It must have been the same clairvoyants who imagined we would be fast-forwarding through commercials to watch our favorite shows, at our favorite time, without running to the store to buy more VHS tapes (thank you TiVo).

Today, customers are in control more than ever. This forces companies and their marketing agencies to work harder and smarter; in many cases, with much less success. Because of our current environment, the business community continues to talk about branding as if it were a saving grace. Every ad agency and marketing firm professes to do branding and many try to put their own spin on how it is delivered. What this does is complicate the reality of this overused and under-implemented strategy approach. I am here to explain to you that branding is really not so complex.

5.1 Branding Is Not as Complicated as It Seems

Branding is not a complicated process, unless you sit down with three different advertising agencies and ask them for their perspective on how to build a brand. Then it becomes scary as hell! Each one will talk about the need to be incredibly creative, yet subtle, in getting your message across. Advertising folks will share their insights on building emotional connections with your audience, delivering self-expressive benefits and — here is my favorite — getting everyone in the company to drink the same Kool-Aid. Each agency will take you down a similar path with slight twists and turns. Most business leaders walk out of these meetings feeling overwhelmed, excited, and ready to allocate their marketing budget into empty strategies and tactics led by glossy paper and clever messaging. **UGH!**

*"I hate this
customer service
Kool-Aid!"*

*"Then don't drink it.
Instead why don't you just
stay focused on doing great
service for our customers?"*

Three reasons advertising and marketing firms that promise
creativity, emotional connections, and getting all employees
"drinking the same Kool-Aid" can't or won't do what they say:

1. **They make money selling paper.** How do advertising firms
   make their money? By selling creative ideas that are printed,
   distributed, or posted on the web. (Oh yeah, they also make
   a lot money marking up advertising space.) How many
   creative ideas do you need throughout the year? Not many.
   How many do they want to sell you? Tons! You can see where
   this is going …

2. **Creative people want to be creative, not practical.** The power of
   the idea should be measured in the result achieved. Many of the
   creative folks employed by your marketing and/or advertising
   partner are simply not business-minded enough to provide the
   most rational and practical business-driven results with respect
   to your brand-building needs.

3. **Posters, mouse pads, and tchotchkes don't sell ideas.**
People sell ideas. Trying to communicate a creative idea
requires making an impact on the belief system of an
individual. Creative is cool, but it will not influence beliefs if
employees know the truth about what happens behind the
scenes. Building a sustainable emotional connection through a
pretty picture is damn near impossible!

*A brand is built from the inside out
by people who use systems and follow processes
to deliver amazing customer experiences.*

5.2 Don't Brand for the Neighborhood

Don't let your marketing partner or ad agency brand you for the neighborhood.

Let me share a story about a friend's company (not my company,
really — it's a friend's company). This company is a large retail
bakery that had plans to franchise throughout the country. From
cakes and pies to muffins, donuts, and gourmet coffees, this
company had it all in the bakery business.

The company leaders believed they needed to brand their business
as the "One-stop Shop" in order to compete with the grocery
chains in the market. So what did they do? You guessed it — large
investments in marketing and advertising in order to get the brand
and associated messages out there. Countless advertisements in
print, on radio, and on TV. Glossy brochures, mailings, and endless
attempts at public relations. And a leadership team
determined to get the messages out to customers
and prospective customers. The messages focused
on delivering emotional, self-expressive (puke), and
functional benefits. They included:

BRAND CHALLENGE

*"Our sales and
marketing depart-
ments tend to make
promises that we
can't always keep."*

• We're passionate about quality — only the best for
you and your family.

- Count on us for amazing customer service — you are important to us and we'll prove it.

- We are your "One-stop Shop," making your life easier.

What great promises! Here is my take on promises straight from the heart, mind, and mouth of a 4-year-old. Recently, my mother (an incredibly reliable and doting grandmother) set a date to make cookies with my daughter, Katie. My mother forgot that she had a doctor's appointment at the same time she promised to bake cookies. Katie was not pleased when grandma delivered the news. She looked right at her and said, "Nonnie, you promised we could make cookies today. A promise is a promise and if you break it, it's a lie." What wonderful insight from a 4-year-old mind. Now back to my example …

If this store really did have a wide selection of products, quality that was second to none, and people who would provide great customer service, then why wouldn't I shop there? The problem was "One-stop Shop" was one-stop short of reality.

Okay, here comes the analogy — the part about branding for the neighborhood. My friend's company painted the white picket fence. They mowed the lawn, planted flowers, painted the house and shutters, and put in a nice new asphalt driveway. In essence, they created amazing curbside appeal. The house looked great! And made the neighbors (fellow company leaders) proud!

Then reality set in. Could the company fulfill the marketing and advertising promises it made? In most cases, no, because the inside of the house didn't get the same attention as the outside. My friend's company couldn't deliver passion for quality with mediocre supplies and employees who didn't pay attention to the details. Customers couldn't experience amazing customer service from unhappy employees. And customers couldn't get the promised "one-stop shopping" because the company had inventory challenges and back orders on products.

SOLUTION

"Stop allowing your branding efforts to be siloed in the marketing department. Focus on the operational processes and people training necessary to deliver the promises you want to make. When you have that figured out, then make your promises!"

This approach of branding for the neighborhood may feel good as you develop new logos and taglines, throw together a glossy brochure, update the Web site, and see your name featured in an ad campaign. But branding for the neighbors is superficial. You paint the house, plant the flowers, and look great from a distance. But the inside of your home is telling a very different story.

Branding for the neighborhood works only if you don't want the neighbors to actually come inside.

The good feeling of fixing up your appearance won't last when the quarterly financial numbers are due, the stress level on the shop floor is higher than ever, and your top two employees decide to quit.

*You can put lipstick on a pig,
but it's still a pig.*

The pig is a simple metaphor to prove one point: a profitable and sustainable brand must be built from the inside out through people, operational processes, and programs.

Business leaders are generally smart people, but not so much when it comes to brand strategy. I've shared this idea countless times and everyone always seems to *know* everything about people and processes being necessary for success. The problem is they're not doing it. There's a big difference between knowing and doing, and many business leaders are without a clue about the power of doing their brand promises versus just saying them. As you continue to read this book, don't tell yourself, "I know how to deliver on our brand promises." Rather, challenge yourself to answer, "How good are we at doing them?"

There's a big difference between knowing and doing.

5.3 Responsible Marketing

Let me make one thing perfectly clear: Advertising will not build you a brand that your employees can deliver for your customers.

Advertising and marketing programs are the tools most marketers use to try to build product-based and organization-wide brands. The belief has traditionally been that if you have the right message and a good product, they will work together to engage consumers and educate them enough to encourage purchase behaviors. The reality is that advertising and marketing can very well be effective at creating awareness and telling people about products and services, yet over time it becomes more and more ineffective at making an impact on building the brand. Because of this, executives are left in precarious situations in which they find it difficult to prove their marketing efforts are responsibly generating top-line growth and bottom-line results.

Going back to Truth #3: *If You Think You Know Your Brand Image You're Probably Wrong*, keep in mind that consumers have desired outcomes that they are trying to accomplish. In all likelihood, unless they believe a product or service will help them reach those outcomes, they won't purchase, or at the very least, not more than once. So if you're a marketing-savvy leader, you must demonstrate extreme caution. You must recognize that marketing executives who believe they can create awareness with vague (or creative) advertising that ignores customers' desired outcomes will only lead you to a dead end. They will take you down an irresponsible path that will turn into an endless race with competitors who probably have similarly obscure and undefined brand messages and experiences.

Truth
NUMBER

5

Marketing and Advertising Can Kill Your Brand

Solution

"Stay focused on desired outcomes of customers and the experiences you can deliver to help them be more successful."

Of course, there are times when generating awareness with clever and catchy advertising programs can become a viable component of the overall brand strategy. For instance, when customers have an aspirational job to accomplish and their desired outcome can be fulfilled by purchasing your product or service. For example, luxury car manufacturers have successfully sold cars by focusing on aspiration. Some individuals purchase a BMW because they aspire to be recognized as an affluent person who loves to drive high-performance vehicles.

On some rare occasions (and I mean very rare), humor can be used effectively to build awareness of a brand. For example, the Geico Gecko is a creative little creature that makes you laugh during very witty commercials (sometimes I won't TiVo through these commercials because they're so funny). In this case, Geico needs you to pick up the phone so they can fulfill their promise to try and save you money on car insurance in 15 minutes or less. While this advertising campaign appears to be successful in creating awareness, the real brand-building happens when they get you on the phone. Geico has a system in place and its employees are trained to deliver a polite, efficient, and money-saving experience. Without the infrastructure behind the witty commercials, the Geico brand would falter.

However, for every successful instance in which marketing and advertising is effectively applied, there are probably tens of thousands of others that have little to show for the money and resources that marketers have thrown at them. In these cases, advertising and external marketing are doing more harm than good — killing the brand before it even gets a chance to delight customers by fulfilling their desired outcomes.

Executives and marketers who believe that creating awareness and recall through advertising and marketing are simply falling into a trap formed by the advertising and marketing people who ultimately win big by selling paper and media — paper in the form of brochures and collateral campaigns including the Web, and media in the form of TV, video, billboard, and radio. All of these media have their place. But in the current competitive marketplace, where customers are tuning out more each day, media's role has dramatically changed. Agencies must become more effective when dealing with the great customer tune-out that is pervasive in our market today.

5.4 The Great Customer Tune-out

Increasingly, customers control the media. With thousands of messages from companies vying for our attention each day, consumers have learned to tune out the irrelevant and will only sometimes catch those messages that align with the desired outcomes they are seeking to achieve. If this is true, then mass marketing's transition to a more personalized approach is not only a good idea, but a requirement for building a branded experience.

One might argue (and I would agree) that mass marketing is absolutely, clinically dead. Large traditional advertisers have been getting on board for years, trying to find ways to create a more personalized approach to targeting consumers through Web sites and product placements in media and entertainment venues. Have you noticed the Coca-Cola cups front and center on *American Idol*? You have if you have ever watched *American Idol*. How about the Motorola headsets being worn by coaches on the sidelines of NFL games? Some product placements are more obvious than others. Like the AT&T Phone-a-Friend on the game show *Who Wants to be a Millionaire*. No, product placement is not a new concept. Remember the lovable alien, E.T., back in 1982? He loved Reese's Pieces. But today, product placement is being done more aggressively, more often, and more strategically than ever before. Why? Because it is becoming one of the more effective ways to reach the customer who has tuned out. It's like a sneak attack that is discovered only after it's too late. As consumers, we have not yet figured out a way to block these product placement messages. But over time, we will.

One of my favorite product placements comes at the end of a NASCAR race. I love to watch the winner crawl out of the car window after a five hour race and hold up a Coke or Pepsi. Can you imagine driving for five hours in a hot, sweaty car and then having to drink a soda to replenish your body fluids? A water might work just fine. These actors (I mean drivers) hold up their bottles of soda in a celebratory toast and don't put them down until the TV interview is complete. They might even fake a sip every now and then just to make us consumers think they are really enjoying their thirst-quenching soda. Ridiculous! Hey Coca-Cola, why don't you invest in the Dasani Bottled Water 500?

If you don't want consumers to tune out, make sure your product appeals to their desired outcomes. In addition, make the approach to delivering the message as personalized and targeted as possible. For instance, Xerox personalized its marketing materials with a campaign targeted at commercial printers. Xerox sent 5,000 lunch boxes to printers, each with personalized marketing materials inside. The lunch box was decorated with the tagline, "Eat your competition's lunch."

It was a clever campaign that I'm sure got the attention of the commercial printer buyers. However, for it to have been successful in generating a response and building the Xerox brand, the messages inside must have been tailored to the desired outcomes the commercial printer was trying to achieve.

Don't think for a minute that you can personalize a campaign by slapping a name on it and dressing it up with pretty colors and pictures to get the consumers' attention. Consumers today are all too familiar with receiving marketing messages personalized with their names. Now they're looking to see immediate relevance to their desired outcomes. If they don't see those elements, they will TUNE YOU OUT!

5.5 Nobody's Paying Attention. Now What? (Ducks, Puppets, and Talking Squirrels Are Not the Answer)

It has always amazed me to see what great lengths some companies will go to in trying to gain the attention of consumers. I'll laugh at a funny advertisement and attempt to figure out what the company is trying to convey. Then I'll make note of what a complete waste of time and money I believe the company is spending. I'll wonder who the marketing genius is behind the foolish efforts.

When I meet a prospective client, partner, or employee, I find it helpful to begin my discussion about branding by sharing with them my favorite *Dilbert* cartoon by Scott Adams. This cartoon clarifies what branding is all about by using the power of opposite thinking.

As a business leader, you can read this cartoon and immediately relate to the craziness that some marketing professionals bring to the table. While the marketing executives are the largest culprit, Scott Adams does a great job of ensuring we see that business leaders are just as susceptible to the ridiculous logic.

Do you remember the sock puppet from Pets.com? Do you remember the experiences you or anyone else had with Pets.com before it crumbled? Enough said.

Then there's the Aflac Duck. Do you find Aflac's commercial to be entertaining? You should. They are. The duck was introduced in 2000 and by 2004 awareness of the Aflac brand had grown from 12 percent to 90 percent. So what! Name recognition alone will not cut it in today's competitive environment. A survey of

1,000 consumers done in October 2003 by Bantam Group, a research firm in Atlanta, found that 60 percent of respondents said they weren't exactly sure what Aflac Insurance was. In addition, a telephone poll of 600 consumers done in April 2004 found that about half of the respondents said the current advertising doesn't explain what Aflac is. Tell me, how can the Aflac Duck be considered a responsible advertising and marketing approach if the audience doesn't understand if it's even relevant to their needs? Yes, the commercials are funny. Yes, they create awareness. No, they don't spark purchase behaviors.

In contrast, think about the Energizer Bunny. This character has become an icon in America. The commercials are funny and at times a bit annoying. Yet, when it comes to product endorsement, the bunny sparks interest and believability. Consumers want their products to work for longer periods of time without having to change the batteries. In order to achieve their desired outcome of longer life usage, they are going to **hire a battery to do the job!** The Energizer Bunny instills confidence, infuses a bit of humor, and is relevant to consumers. Hats off to the folks at Energizer for sticking with this campaign decade after decade. There is no reason to change it. I hope my kids' kids get to experience the Energizer Bunny in the first few decades of their lifetime.

Most companies don't have the discipline to stick with a campaign as Energizer has done. Why? Because of marketing executives and business leaders like the one in the *Dilbert* cartoon — individuals who get bored with their company's message long (often decades) before consumers do.

Advertising agencies are always grappling with the challenge of creating ads that entertain while also imparting relevant information about a product or service. Why does it work for the Energizer Bunny and not the Aflac Duck? Because the former recognizes that consumers have a job to do and clearly conveys the message of how the product can help them do it.

It's not realistic to say that no one is paying attention anymore. Consumers are paying attention more than ever to those things that are relevant and meaningful to them.

The advertising industry has been hit hard by agency downsizing and closings. What are agencies to do? I'll tell you. Agencies should stay focused on the task of positioning products and services in the minds of consumers. To do so in today's world requires a shift in thinking away from meaningless mass marketing to more strategic promotional programs and entertainment-oriented advertising. Every ounce of energy that an agency exudes for a client should be focused on doing three things great:

1. Conducting necessary research to understand the target customer and their desired outcomes (not something that "creatives" typically get passionate about; in fact, they tend to avoid it).

2. Establishing meaningful points of difference for their clients based on target customer research (real difference that can be delivered through their people and processes).

3. Developing strategic and creative tactics to engage, inspire, and motivate consumers to buy more of their client's stuff, positioning their products and services in the minds of consumers (creativity that is on-strategy; not creativity just to be creative).

If agencies don't focus on the above three areas, they'll continue to kill brands (and marketing budgets) before we, as consumers, even get a chance to understand what the potential might have been.

5.6 The Stupidest Promotion Ever

In 2005, General Motors decided to run what I believe is the most stupid, most brand-diminishing promotion in the history of our world. With one swoop of stupidity, GM almost certainly put a dent in its corporate brand and all of its automobile brands. On the following page are some headlines from articles highlighting the impact of GM's actions.

"After Autos' Big Summer, Sales Continue to Weaken"

"GM to End 401k Match"

General Motors Corporation distributed a packet this week to 36,000 U.S. salaried employees announcing that it would suspend matching contributions to 401k retirement plans for white-collar workers. GM also said it would reduce severance benefits.

"GM Shares Sink to 23-Year Low as Woes Mount"

GM may be dethroned as biggest maker of autos.

"Toyota Could Make GM No. 2 in 2006"

Analysts say it's just a matter of time before the Japanese automaker overtakes struggling U.S. rival General Motors as the world's top automaker.

I would have loved to have been in the boardroom the day someone at GM came up with the idea to give everyone "The Employee Discount." Mark my words, the employee discount promotion will go on record as the stupidest ever.

Do you know anyone who works for GM? If you do, then you know how special the employee discount is for them. I used to live next door to a guy who worked for GM. His discount was quite a perk for him, his friends, and his family. He was able to buy a few cars each year and receive amazing deals on the price. He offered me the opportunity the same year he purchased a few cars on behalf of other family and friends. So, in a day and age when employee perks were rare and finding ways to delight your employees was more difficult than ever, GM had a golden ticket with the employee discount. If you worked for the company, you got to purchase a car at a price far below what the average John or Jane Doe paid.

At least, that was the benefit to employees before the summer of 2005. GM must have been in a situation in which its dealers were in sudden need of moving cars. I can just imagine the scene where the genius marketing executive said, "I know, let's give everyone the employee discount. The price will be so low that those cars will jump out of the lots." This decision was probably made with a complete disregard to the short- and long-term impact on employees of the company.

If GM was building a superior car and positioning its brand in powerful ways, it might not have even been in the situation. But it was in the situation and giving away the employee discount must have seemed like the best way out. I think it will turn out to be the worst mistake ever and will take decades to recover from. If it ever recovers at all!

Here's why:

First, GM may have alienated its entire employee base, diminishing the value of one of the best perks some employees are offered. By giving the employee discount to everyone, GM was saying, "Hey employees, you're not so special anymore. Anyone can have your special perk." At the very least, GM should have considered providing the 36,000 employees (who just lost their 401k match) the opportunity to deliver the employee discount through a more aggressive program. Maybe they could have offered them the same incredible incentive to pass on to anyone they want. If I worked for GM, I could have walked up to a stranger on the street and given them a coupon for $5,000 off a GM car. Then, for each coupon used, GM could have repurposed the enormous ad budget and paid a bonus to the employees. Or, at the very least, it could have lessened the decrease in the 401k. This would have sparked greater employee pride, put more money in their pockets, and still led to increased car sales.

Second, GM probably alienated all of its most loyal customers. Why? Because if you are the owner of a GM car that you purchased three years ago for $30,000 and expected to trade in for $17,000, think again. Now GM might be selling that same model car brand new for $24,000, in all likelihood greatly diminishing the value of your trade-in. The negative impact on resale compared to the foreign competition will be felt for years to come.

Third, I believe GM dramatically lowered the perceived value of its autos when it participated in a large discounting activity such as the employee discount. It diminished brand value across the board for new customers, old customers, and the most important GM customer: the employees.

So GM, with one promotion, alienated its employee base and its existing customer base on top of diminishing its total brand value.

Want more proof that GM is headed down the wrong road? In comparing November sales from 2004 and 2005, GM sales were down 11.4 percent while Toyota was up 5.6 percent — a 17 percent differential in one month. Is this an aberration or a sign of things to come? If I were a betting man, I would not bet one dime on GM.

Why didn't Toyota follow suit? Because Toyota is building superior cars that are perceived to be more valuable in the minds of American consumers. That is why Toyota will soon sit atop the auto world with record sales in the years ahead while GM will be finding ways to perform disaster relief from its own stupid promotion.

GM, a perfect example of how advertising and marketing can kill your brand!

A few final thoughts. Marketing and advertising won't build brands for products, services, or organizations. Experiences delivered in alignment with desired outcomes build powerful, sustainable brands. Therefore, be leery of any individual or company that says they are selling you branding or a brand strategy. Make sure what they are selling is really what you need. The majority of vendors who say they are selling branding are selling nothing more than pithy marketing messages and pretty pictures.

In the following chapter (Truth #6), I will provide the framework for building an actionable brand strategy that takes you miles beyond logos, taglines, and creative marketing ideas.

Truth #6: *Behaviors and Experiences Make the Invisible Visible* covers the foundation for the entire *Achieving Brand Integrity* approach to branding. It provides direction for building a brand strategy. The Ideas Into Action section provides several of the necessary tools and steps to take to engage your team in the brand-building process.

Truth
NUMBER

5

Marketing and Advertising Can Kill Your Brand

Truth
NUMBER

Behaviors and Experiences Make the Invisible Visible

Truth
NUMBER

6

Behaviors and
Experiences
Make the
Invisible
Visible

....

IDEAS ····⟩ ACTION

1 Build a Brand Lens and Operationally Define Brand Concepts	2 Conduct an Experience Audit	3 Create, Prioritize, and Implement Experiences

Truth
NUMBER

6

Behaviors and
Experiences
Make the
Invisible
Visible

WARNING! If you are not completely serious about building a brand strategy, then be careful reading Truth #6. Doing so will get you fired up and ready to create a truly brand-driven business. This part of the book will guide you through the process of creating a brand strategy from defining the concepts that make up your brand to documenting the behaviors and experiences required to do it. I will provide you with the tools required to begin building your brand strategy with your team.

You'll notice I said "with your team." Great brand strategies need viewpoints and commitment from several individuals on your team. Picking a brand team is easy. Choose cross-functional representation and include people who are visionary, willing to share their ideas, and (most important) those who are respected by their peers. Why the respected folks? Because they will be the champions of this strategy from the moment the horse is out of the barn. You want them on board in order to help stimulate buy-in from others throughout the company.

But, before we get started:

6.1 Your Brand Is Not One Big Idea

Some practitioners refer to the brand and a brand strategy as one big idea that you can build a campaign or business around. From a strategic/business-focused perspective, this is quite simply NOT TRUE! A brand strategy must be held accountable to deliver increases in employee productivity, customer loyalty, and sales. One big idea cannot be.

A big idea is just that, an idea. Once a big idea fizzles out over time, smart marketing and creative folks come up with another big idea. Then the advertising agency comes up with another. And another. (You see where this is going.)

For leaders who thrive on the glitz and glamour of advertising agencies' dog and pony shows, the one big idea approach may seem entertaining. However, for the everyday employee, the big idea game is nothing more than a "flavor of the month" that provides ammunition for already cynical employees and disengages most others.

In Truth #1, I stated that *a brand is the sum total of every experience a customer has with your company and its products and services — a sum total that customers begin to think of as the promise you make.*

The same definition holds true for employees, partners, and vendors, as well.

Also in Truth #1, I shared the truth that a brand strategy is the ultimate business strategy. If you buy into any of my philosophy (which you must or you wouldn't still be reading), you will clearly see that a brand can't possibly be equivalent to one big idea. The brand is the end result of the execution of a brand strategy (the process of aligning what we say with what we do so that we can positively influence what customers think). The brand is not a means to an end. It is the outcome of a well-executed strategy — a result that drives organizational culture and leads to tremendous loyalty among employees and customers.

> *The brand is the end result of the execution of a brand strategy.*

While the concept of organizational branding may still seem vague, it should be easy to understand when put in the context of more familiar organizational development initiatives (you know, the ones that typically provide short-term insight and inspiration and very little long-term value because they aren't easily do-able for leaders and employees). I'm talking about business fluff[1] (and it is fluff) like mission and vision statements, core values, and business principles. And — here is my favorite — pillars of success.

1 Business fluff: Things people get excited about but could do just as well without.

Guess who the following core values belonged to as defined in a 2000 annual report:

- Communication
- Respect
- Integrity
- Excellence

Truth
NUMBER
6

Behaviors and
Experiences
Make the
Invisible
Visible

It could be lots of companies, but in this case it was Enron! Have I made my point?

Enron is not alone in its quest to add meaning to its organization without being able to provide any substance. You'll find that most of corporate America is filled with organizations that publicly (or at least internally to employees) promote their core values, mission, and/or principles with a complete disregard for how to actually engage, inspire, and motivate employees to do them. These values become nothing more than empty statements and claims that generate employee cynicism while undermining management's credibility.

Has your company been guilty of empty gestures with respect to core values, mission statements, brand promises, or principles? Have you defined what the words are behind your values only to leave out the definition of how to do them through behaviors at work?

If so, don't sweat it. Read on …

Company efforts in these activities are often fruitless because they lead to a collection of words with little conceptual meaning. A brand consists of concepts that need to be defined based on who, what, why, when, where, and **how**. I emphasize the how because this is the part that is most important, but often gets the least attention from organizational leaders.

BRAND CHALLENGE

"We've got a mission statement but can't seem to get employees to do it."

I'm about to begin explaining the steps required to start building a brand strategy. You'll find this to be very exciting. You and your leadership team will develop brand concepts that define who you are. As you begin this step, remember that employees must be held accountable for doing the concepts. Truth #8: *Gaining Buy-in Is the Only Way to Execute a Brand Strategy* will take you down the pathway of integrating your concepts into your employees' job profiles and evaluation processes. I want you to be thinking about the integration into employee jobs as you read the remainder of this chapter. Please avoid thinking about ways to market and sell the brand. Keep in mind, reaching *Brand Integrity* is accomplished from doing, not saying.

6.2 Building the Brand Lens

As we work through the *Achieving Brand Integrity* process, we place these concepts in a visual called the Brand Lens.[2] The Brand Lens houses the brand concepts (values) that you want your company to be known for. You notice I said *concepts* (plural).

2 Brand Lens: A visual representation of your company's desired brand image. The few concepts you want to be known for and therefore must *do* for employees and customers.

We're The Experts

Innovative Products and Services

Amazing Customer Service

Operational Excellence

A Great Place To Work

A sample Brand Lens

Again, your brand does not consist of one big idea. It consists of a series of ideas that if executed upon can differentiate your company in the market and make your company more profitable. At first they are just "invisible" words on paper. Consider them to be lousy taglines as they are not necessarily creative slogans. However, they are the foundation of the brand that can be defined from an operational perspective.

SOLUTION

"Define the behaviors required to do your mission and hold employees accountable through performance assessments and evaluations."

In the sample Brand Lens, you will find the types of brand concepts that many companies create. The brand strategy process must guide you through operationally defining how to deliver on these concepts through your people and processes. To do so, you must uncover the behaviors and experiences necessary to make them visible.

Truth
NUMBER

6

Behaviors and
Experiences
Make the
Invisible
Visible

Even with great concepts outlined in your Brand Lens, values statement, vision, mission, principles, or as part of a brand identity, the ideas are still invisible and left to the interpretation of each leader and employee. Think about Enron. Each leader probably had his or her own beliefs about what respect and integrity looked like — some legal, and some, well, maybe not so legal.

Brand Lens concepts can be categorized into three types:

1. Values-based

Brand concepts that represent closely held beliefs of the company's leaders — core beliefs never to be compromised for convenience or short-term gain.

2. Price-to-Entry

Brand concepts that are required to successfully compete in the industry. The minimum standards for employee behavior, these brand concepts alone will rarely differentiate your company.

3. Aspirational

Brand concepts that would enable a company to compete more successfully but are not consistently delivered (or not delivered at all). Aspirational brand concepts typically require the most resources during a brand strategy implementation because the programs, processes, and systems are not yet in place to deliver them. In addition, the gap between saying and doing is usually greatest for aspirational concepts.

Your brand consists of several ideas. The challenge is determining and defining what else. What else is your company known for? What else could your company be known for? What else should your company be known for? These are questions that I hope you will ponder as you read the remainder of this book.

6.3 Why Your Brand Is Invisible

Even if you've figured out your company's Brand Lens concepts, keep in mind that they are still invisible. Don't think for a minute that you're done with developing your brand. You're not even close. You've arrived at the gate, but the race has not even started.

WHAT DOES IT MEAN TO HAVE AN INVISIBLE BRAND CONCEPT? WHY IS IT SO BAD?

A brand strategy practitioner (okay, I'm referring to me) will tell you that an invisible brand concept jeopardizes companies because it leads to a culture in which:

1. Employees create their own meaning for the brand concept.

2. Employees do the concept in their own way — behave the way they see fit to bring the concept to their reality.

3. Productivity, customer loyalty, and sales opportunities decrease.

4. Desperate leaders falsely communicate to inflate stock price, disregard integrity while "cooking the books," and disrespect employees and shareholders while stealing right from their pockets. (Okay, last Enron jab. I promise.)

IS YOUR BRAND INVISIBLE?

Are your Brand Lens concepts invisible to your employees, customers, and stakeholders? Your answer to this question will clearly be yes if each employee in your company does not know the brand concepts he or she is accountable for and how to behave in ways to bring those brand concepts to life.

Truth
NUMBER

6

Behaviors and Experiences Make the Invisible Visible

A strategy without execution is like a Lamborghini with flat tires. You can't go anywhere.

Think about it. Do your employees really know the actions (behaviors) required for them to bring your company's brand to life? Do they have autonomy to bring

101

it to life in their own way? If so, your brand is still invisible. Very invisible!

Before I go into detail on how to make the brand visible, let's first review how brand concepts get stuck being invisible. The reality is that all brands start out invisible (like I said, they are just ideas on paper). Nothing more than mission statements, core values, or business principles. A few catchy words with little substance or know-how. They don't have to stay that way, though most unfortunately do.

Truth
NUMBER

6

Behaviors and
Experiences
Make the
Invisible
Visible

WHAT ARE THE CAUSES OF THE INVISIBLE BRAND?

Here are the six causes of the invisible brand:

1. **No belief system exists.** Employees don't understand the beliefs that make the brand concepts important to them in their day-to-day jobs. They lack the ability to see how delivering the brand concepts makes work more meaningful for them or generates more success for the company as a whole.

2. **Benefits are misunderstood.** Employees lack understanding of the meaningful benefits that customers are seeking and how doing a particular brand concept can lead to benefits being delivered.

3. **Poor attitudes.** Beliefs power attitudes. A weak belief system coupled with a lack of understanding true customer benefits leads to frustration, which becomes evident in employee attitudes.

4. **Employees choose their own behaviors.** Employees have the autonomy to deliver the brand in their own way. For instance, if each employee has different expectations of what Excellent Customer Service looks like, then naturally they will each do it differently.

5. **Experiences are not managed.** Customer experiences become erratic and are inconsistently delivered from employee to employee and from day to day. The brand stays invisible and often contrary concepts are melded into the minds of employees and customers.

102

6. Desired business results are not pervasively understood.
Employees do not really understand the business goals and objectives that are to be achieved. Therefore, they don't know if the company — or their own performance — is on track for success.

Let me try to sum up some of the above points.

Beliefs drive attitudes. Attitudes drive behaviors. Behaviors drive experiences for others. Those experiences lead to a business result (more or less productivity, loyalty, and/or sales).

If you don't like the business result your company is achieving, look at the experiences your employees are delivering. If you don't like the experiences, look at the behaviors. If you don't like the behaviors, look at the beliefs that your company has communicated and tried to instill in its employees. If clearly defined beliefs have not been established, then you have work to do. Keep reading …

WHO CAUSES THE INVISIBLE BRAND?

Good question. Nothing like placing a little blame! The answer should be quite obvious. The CEO, President, and senior-level leaders are to blame. As the ultimate people in charge, C-level leaders are the biggest culprits. They are also the best ones to start the process of fixing the invisible brand, making it visible.

Here is the prescription (brand strategy development model) for Making the Invisible Visible with respect to your company's brand. This brand strategy approach will ensure that what you say is what you do, so that you can influence what customers (and employees) think.

Truth
NUMBER

6

Behaviors and
Experiences
Make the
Invisible
Visible

Making the Invisible Visible

See, it's all starting to come together, isn't it?

The formula for making this model work is quite simple. Unfortunately, most companies just don't seem to be willing to do the hard work that it takes to build a brand-driven business. Why? Because while it seems simple, it is definitely not easy. Sometimes you get stuck.[3] You get stuck because you are trying something new. You hit roadblocks. Everyone on the team has different agendas, different perceptions about right and wrong, and different beliefs about which direction to proceed.

3 Stuck: In a rut.
Good ideas
with little
consensus.
Inability to
move forward.

Sometimes just broaching the subject leads to everyone getting stuck. Now the leadership team is stuck. Now the entire company is in a rut. But being stuck is a temporary state. You don't have to stay that way. You, as one of the leaders, know what needs to get done.

6.4 Make Your Brand Mean Something

The most successful leaders understand they must win the hearts and minds of employees in a way that is honest and authentic. The best way to get started in winning hearts and minds is to involve employees in the process of creating the company's brand concepts.

I am not suggesting that you bring your leaders together to create a series of principles, core values, and a mission statement and then dress it up with fancy branding terminology like brand identity, brand concepts, brand picture, or brand vision.

I am suggesting that you bring your leaders together to define the meaning behind your brand. Creating meaning behind a brand concept won't make it totally visible, but it will provide the first required step for making your brand real.

If you are really going to make your brand mean something, you need to begin thinking of your employees as the "living brand." They are the individuals who collectively bring the brand to life. To leverage this potential, leaders must devote a great deal of time and energy to hiring, training, and developing employees so they can understand the brand, its promises, and core values.

WHAT IF ...

What if you as a leader started the process of shifting energy and resources away from pretentious marketing messages that tell what the brand is and does and repurposed your efforts toward grooming employees in their commitment to understanding the brand beliefs and doing the brand behaviors?

Do you think this would make the brand mean something to your employees? You bet!

For those of you who may not be fully bought in yet, consider this: if you have a brand promise, core values, or a crafty mission statement that communicates to employees and customers, you may be doing more harm than good for your company. This will most likely be the case if your employees don't know how to deliver the promises made. Going back to the Excellent Customer Service example, if you set an expectation for superior service but haven't figured out how to deliver it, you may be better off telling customers to expect mediocre service. At least then they won't be disappointed by what they get.

6.5 Can You See It? Is It Visible?

4 Operational-
izing the
brand is
the process
of defining
what the
brand means
as well as
how to do
it through
employee
behaviors
and the
delivery of
customer
experiences.

To successfully make a brand visible is to operationally define it. By operationalizing[4] the brand, you are in essence bringing it to life through your employees via your systems, processes, and programs. This requires taking the brand well beyond the executive suite and far past the marketing department to all parts of your infrastructure so it becomes an integral part of doing business in your company.

When your company leaders see the brand as a strategy that drives your company, then you will be on your way to becoming a brand-driven business — a business where the brand drives the success of all other strategies and initiatives including the strategic plan (the business strategy). The brand becomes more visible as it comes to be considered the necessary driver and/or key influencer for pricing, distribution, sales, and other strategies. All of these strategies need direction from the brand strategy in order to fully realize their brand potential.

As stated in Truth #1, the brand strategy is the ultimate business strategy. The above-mentioned strategies are sub-components of the overall brand strategy.

To make your brand visible, employees must know how to take appropriate action on clearly defined beliefs. This approach infuses accountability into the workforce and creates a shared expectation for consistent, visible, on-brand behaviors and experiences.

BELIEFS ARE INVISIBLE, BUT YOU CAN SEE BEHAVIORS

Not only are behaviors visible, they are also measurable. Most behaviors are observable to others. Therefore, infusing them into job descriptions and the evaluation process provides a great way to educate, gain commitment, and ensure the right actions are taken.

Uncovering behaviors that are aligned with your brand concepts will also help to ensure that employees are doing the right things, not just doing things right.

As stated earlier, if you do not go through the process of operationally defining the brand (which includes documenting the required behaviors for delivery) then you are taking the risk of allowing each employee to define success in their own terms.

So if behaviors are what employees do in their daily interactions and tasks, what exactly are experiences?

6.6 Experiences Deliver Results

Experiences are planned events that are orchestrated by employees. They are the tactical aspects of the brand strategy that once delivered should drive success of at least one of the three key result areas:

Truth
NUMBER

6
Behaviors and
Experiences
Make the
Invisible
Visible

1. Increased productivity of employees.

2. Stronger customer loyalty.

3. Increased sales to customers.

Throughout this book I've continued to reiterate what I believe are the three most important key result areas for 99 percent of businesses in the world. Think of them as the key performance metrics to measure all brand-building efforts. Productivity, loyalty, and sales ... what else really matters as a result?

As Joseph Pine II and James H. Gilmore state in their book *The Experience Economy*, "work is theatre and every business is a stage." If you haven't read this book, I absolutely recommend that you do. Understanding their unique perspective on how business is done today and will continue to be done in the future is imperative for any company that truly wants to dominate its industry.

Pine and Gilmore go on to say that all companies "stage" experiences whenever they want to engage customers and connect with them in a personal, memorable way. Please note that it is not about entertaining customers, it's about engaging them in a way that is relevant to their needs and wants.

An important point to note is that experiences are delivered by employees, products, or services. Therefore, a system of behaviors must be put in place to ensure that the experience is able to get to the customer through those employees, products, or services. Behaviors drive the experiences.

Sometimes my clients get confused between a behavior and an experience. I tell them an experience has to meet two major criteria: it must be a preplanned, consistently executed initiative or program and it must provide a meaningful benefit to the customer.

Pine and Gilmore seem to share a similar belief about *doing* versus *saying* your brand message in their report, *The Experience IS the Marketing.* They state, "People have become relatively immune to messages targeted *at* them. The way to reach your customers is to create an experience *within* them. . . . We are talking about a fundamentally new way of attracting and retaining your customers through creating new experience offerings. It's not about experience marketing, but rather *marketing experiences.*"

Truth
NUMBER

6

Behaviors and
Experiences
Make the
Invisible
Visible

If experiences drive business results, then does it now make sense to create your first-ever experience budget? That's right, a budgeted line item for staging experiences. Take the money right out of your existing marketing budget. Don't be afraid. This approach is working for organizations such as Starbucks, Southwest Airlines, In-N-Out Burger, Amazon.com, Google, and a host of other leading companies. Marketing becomes superfluous as you begin to devise more compelling ways to connect and interact with customers through the delivery of your services and products.

And, if customers receive benefits from experiences, then your pricing strategy should certainly reflect those benefits by rewarding your company with higher margins.

Disney World prides itself on delivering experiences that demonstrate fun, family, and entertainment. To help families experience these concepts, they need to stage a few experiences using their frontline workers. Here is an example I personally experienced when visiting Disney with my wife and daughters.

THE KNOWLEDGEABLE WHITE JUMPSUIT MAN

Optimizing your time in a Disney theme park requires some strategic thinking. Avoiding long lines and getting you and your kids on or into as many attractions as possible within your given time constraint is your main objective. Disney employees know this. That's why when my wife and I looked a little lost and confused as to where to go next, we were approached (yes, approached/sought out/found) by a Disney maintenance man in a white jumpsuit. While this man was dressed and accessorized for cleaning the park, he was actually equipped with much more than a broom and dust pan. Not only was he friendly, professional, and knowledgeable of daily attractions, he knew quite a bit about avoiding long lines.

Truth
NUMBER

6

Behaviors and
Experiences
Make the
Invisible
Visible

"You look like you might need some assistance. May I help you get to your next Disney adventure?" the man asked as he approached us. Naturally, my wife and I obliged. "Your daughters would love the Beauty and the Beast Show that begins in 45 minutes. I would suggest that one of you get in line for that now. Also, in about five minutes, Mickey Mouse will be coming out about 30 feet behind me. Why don't one of you take the kids there and then meet up at the Beauty and the Beast Show line? That way, your kids won't need to wait very long for either attraction." He completed the experience by providing precise directions and a map on how to get to the Beauty and the Beast entrance.

Disney recognizes that their maintenance people are frontline customer touchpoints. Therefore, they should be trained and equipped with the capabilities, skills, and knowledge to be social coordinators. They also realize that positive experiences will be communicated by happy customers to potential new customers.

The average Disney customer would probably tell at least 20 people about that experience. Personally, I have told thousands prior to writing this book. Thank you, Disney, for continuing to orchestrate the great experiences that delight the families you count on. This is one extraordinary example; in your company, an experience might be as simple as remembering a customer's birthday or sending a thank-you card or gift basket.

SOLUTION

"Stop telling them and start showing them. Define the behaviors and experiences you want your people to do. Then make sure these behaviors and experiences are a part of their job description and evaluation."

Who in your organization is the CEO? You know, the Chief Experience Officer who is responsible for managing the delivery of employee and customer experiences.

The brand strategy's purpose is to ensure your company delivers what it says it will deliver, in order to influence what people think. Seems quite obvious that the company will need an individual or a team of individuals to be accountable for overseeing and measuring the implementation of experiences.

Truth
NUMBER

6

Behaviors and
Experiences
Make the
Invisible
Visible

Who in your company should be the Chief Experience Officer? Who should participate on the Brand Leadership Council? The Brand Leadership Council is a group of individuals who are passionate about implementing your brand strategy and demonstrate a willingness and desire to be held accountable.

Experiences must be managed. The execution of a brand strategy depends on it. Once the strategy is created, 90 percent or more of the energy and resources needed to sustain it must focus on measuring the experiences over time. This includes employee experiences that drive productivity: training, development, and behavioral management. It also includes customer experiences that drive loyalty and sales.

Delivering experiences requires, at the least, a small degree of innovation. Innovation is simply the creative act of bringing a new experience to life; a new experience that leads to a quantifiable gain for your company. The key word in this definition is *quantifiable gain*.

Innovating experiences is a simple concept, but rarely easy to do. You need to begin by changing behaviors, and you should begin with those behaviors that touch the customer first. I recommend you map every point of contact between your company and the customer from pre-purchase through purchase and post-purchase to the final stage of relationship building.

Of course this "map" has a name. I call it a Touchpoint Experience Wheel.

Ask yourself: Do these points of contact provide great experiences for our customers? Is there opportunity to do more? If you are delivering experiences, how consistently are you delivering them? Are they strengthening your company's brand image or hindering it?

THE TOUCHPOINT EXPERIENCE WHEEL

The Touchpoint Experience Wheel houses all of the different ways your company's brand interacts with and makes impressions on employees, customers, and other stakeholders (your audiences). You will find that there are many touchpoints that are represented by tactics and behaviors geared to reach an audience. Touchpoints are the starting point for an experience. Remember, to be deemed an experience, it must be consistently delivered and managed.

Each touchpoint is an opportunity to enhance the opinion an audience has about your brand. Touchpoints fall into four quadrants (pre-purchase, purchase, post-purchase, and relationship building). For illustration purposes, I will refer to the Touchpoint Experience Wheel for the customer audience (as opposed to the employee audience).

PRE-PURCHASE: All of the interactions potential customers have with your brand prior to making the decision to do business with your company.

These touchpoints have one primary goal: to generate awareness and consideration. Examples of pre-purchase touchpoints:

• Any form of advertising whether print or media

• Your participation in trade shows

• Your Web site

• Interactive forums and user dialogues

111

When customers are in need of a product or service that you provide, you want them to be aware of who you are and consider you as a candidate for their supplier. Each pre-purchase touchpoint should be designed to shape perceptions and expectations of the brand in ways that are most relevant for the customer. For prospects, pre-purchase touchpoints should help them understand the benefits of the brand versus competitive offerings.

Truth
NUMBER

6

Behaviors and
Experiences
Make the
Invisible
Visible

Most companies have traditionally focused the bulk of their energy and resources to this stage of the customer life cycle. For decades, advertising and marketing firms have made their living selling materials and messages that generate awareness and consideration. My belief is that if touchpoints in the other three quadrants (purchase, post-purchase, and relationship building) are maximized by well-orchestrated experiences, then companies can begin to spend much less time and money on generating awareness.

Traditional ways of generating awareness are becoming more ineffective and in some cases obsolete, yet they remain very expensive. Truth #5: *Marketing and Advertising Can Kill Your Brand* shared many details of old, outdated tactics used to generate awareness. Remember, one of the goals of a brand strategy is to turn your customers into an unpaid marketing department that generates awareness and consideration through endorsements and dramatically decreases the costs of generating awareness.

The goal of the pre-purchase stage is to generate awareness so customers will consider buying your product or service.

PURCHASE: The interactions with customers that take them from considering your products or services to making the purchase. The primary goal of the purchase phase is to help your customer or prospect buy your product or service. The main objective is to instill confidence in customers and help them feel comfortable with the decision to choose your offering over others. Every company has purchase touchpoints that must be managed. Below are a few examples of touchpoints from a professional service firm and a retail store business.

Professional service firm purchase touchpoints:

- Phone greeting
- Initial sales call/meeting
- Follow-up responses to meetings
- Proposal presentation

Retail store purchase touchpoints:

- Customer greeting
- Store physical environment
- Salesperson/clerk assistance
- Customer checkout

Truth
NUMBER

6

Behaviors and
Experiences
Make the
Invisible
Visible

The goal of the purchase stage is to help your customer buy your product or service.

POST-PURCHASE: The customer experience that starts the minute after the "sale" is concluded — a.k.a., the most overlooked opportunity in business today. Post-purchase touchpoints are crucial to enhancing the overall customer experience. Right at the point when a customer may be feeling post-purchase dissonance that they made a wrong decision or that they could have done without the offering, these touchpoints help customers feel good about their decision to do business with your company. These touchpoints provide the greatest opportunity to deliver experiences that drive sustainable growth and profitability. Sticking with our theme of a professional service firm and a retail store, below are a few examples of post-purchase touchpoints.

Professional service firm post-purchase touchpoints:

- Welcome letter
- Project kickoff meeting
- Employee or team introductions

Retail store post-purchase touchpoints:

- Thank-you cards or calls
- Follow-up calls to check on satisfaction
- Product guarantees
- Product education

The goal of the post-purchase stage is to help your customers feel good about their purchase decision.

RELATIONSHIP BUILDING: Interactions that bring active customers closer to being advocates for your brand. The purpose of relationship-building touchpoints is two-fold: retain customer business and stimulate customer referrals. In most cases, if the relationship a customer has with your company and its products and services is not strong, he or she will not continue to be a customer. If this happens, he or she will also be unlikely to refer your company to others. Relationship-building touchpoints feed right back into the pre-purchase touchpoints, building awareness and restarting the customer life cycle.

Truth
NUMBER

6

Behaviors and
Experiences
Make the
Invisible
Visible

The goal of the relationship building stage is to increase customer retention and stimulate referrals.

Professional service firm relationship-building touchpoints:

• Invoices

• Networking events and trade shows

• Delivery of work product

Retail store relationship-building touchpoints:

• Public relations activities

• Loyalty program communications

• Community sponsorships

6.7 Brands Drive Culture

WORK CULTURE: THE WAY WE DO THINGS AROUND HERE!

Internal behaviors and the experiences a company delivers create its culture. If this is the case, one could argue that a brand strategy drives the culture of an organization. To an extent, this is true.

I would like to introduce you to brand magic. It's what happens once you've operationally defined your brand concepts (documenting beliefs, uncovering necessary behaviors, and determining the optimal experiences to deliver). The brand begins to drive behaviors which have an impact on the culture. Within 12 to 18 months, what happens is truly magical: the culture begins to drive the brand. This time frame can be much shorter for smaller companies.

Employees in a brand-driven work culture radiate when they deviate from the expected behaviors. Some employees will find they are not a good fit for the brand culture of the company. They

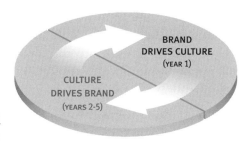

will have their own belief systems that are not in alignment with those of the company. Many will be able to adapt and modify their behaviors. Some will not. Those who cannot adapt will typically act out, making it easier for you to encourage them to test out the job market. Better yet, they opt out, leaving your company to join another one where brand expectations are not set and monitored. In many cases, they will go to your competitors, the ones whose asses you will be kicking by delivering experiences through a motivated, engaged, and inspired workforce!

There is one GREAT way to ensure that you can hold employees accountable for consistently delivering the branded experience of your organization. You must define the specific behaviors for the employees' jobs, integrate those behaviors into their job descriptions, and make sure they conduct self-assessments regularly. In addition, the brand-driven behaviors must be integrated into the annual performance review process. These behaviors make up at least 51 percent of the success any given employee will have with your company. The 51 percent constitutes their personality, attitude, and behaviors that are in alignment with your brand strategy. The other 49 percent represents the knowledge, technical skills, and job-specific capabilities that are required to fulfill the technical/operational side of the job.

The next two Truths will take you down the pathway of learning more about how to integrate the brand strategy into any given job category in your company. Keep reading …

Truth
NUMBER

6

Behaviors and Experiences Make the Invisible Visible

Build a Brand Lens and Operationally Define the Brand Concepts

Gather together a few leaders in your company and engage them in the process of building and defining a Brand Lens.[5] You will need to get them thinking about potential brand concepts that can be operationally defined in the form of beliefs, benefits, and

5 A Brand Lens serves as the platform for housing the concepts that drive your brand strategy. Leaders look through the Brand Lens when making any and all decisions about the company.

We're The Experts
Innovative Products and Services
Amazing Customer Service
Operational Excellence
A Great Place To Work

A sample Brand Lens

behaviors. For each concept, challenge the members of your team to describe the beliefs and benefits that make the concept important to your company and customers. In addition, begin to explore the behaviors required to prove each brand concept. By documenting the behaviors that will bring your brand concepts to life, you will be making the invisible visible. This saying was shared with me by my good friend Bob Rosenfeld. Bob is the Innovator in Residence at the Center for Creative Leadership and is the CEO of Idea Connection Systems, a consulting company that creates systems to release the human potential for organizations. Bob coined the term "making the invisible visible" in the organizational development and innovation field. His concept makes great sense in the branding and business strategy arena. Think about it this way: you can't see someone's beliefs; however, you can see their attitude and

Brand challenge

"Some of my employees are stuck in the 'same old way' we've always done things. They're not willing to change."

behaviors. If behaviors are your beliefs turned into action, then it's safe to say that behaviors are the visible part of your brand. The behaviors lead to the experiences that wow your employees and customers, encouraging them to be more loyal to your company. Thank you, Bob, for opening my eyes to this incredibly simple and very powerful concept.

 For exercises on how to build and operationally define a Brand Lens, go to www.brandintegrity.com/truth6.

After you have completed building and defining your Brand Lens, you will have operationally defined brand concepts. Now you're ready to begin focusing on the experiences delivered to employees and customers that will lead to greater loyalty to your brand.

CONDUCT AN EXPERIENCE AUDIT

An experience audit begins with scanning your current work environment and activities to uncover experiences your company already delivers that are driving perceptions among employees and customers.

Pull together 10 to 20 employees. Form three teams. Choose a captain for each team. Send them off to brainstorm *existing* experiences in their group, trying to uncover experiences that are currently being delivered to influence perceptions of employees and customers.

Once the team captains come back with experiences, bucket them into two categories:

1. Continue experiences

2. Stop experiences

Having the experiences divided into these categories will become valuable as you progress with the brand-building process. If nothing else, it will get your employees thinking about behaviors and experiences that are driving

SOLUTION

"Give them the opportunity to test out the job market."

perceptions — behaviors and experiences that need to be managed if they are to be delivered consistently or stopped because they are harmful.

Finally, provide a "consistency ranking." Rank each experience already being done that the company should continue doing. Be honest. If an experience is rarely done or only done occasionally by a few people, don't sugarcoat how well it is performed.

"Consistency is king."

Truth
NUMBER

6

Behaviors and
Experiences
Make the
Invisible
Visible

For a template for conducting an experience audit and consistency ranking, go to www.brandintegrity.com/truth6 and download the Experience Audit template.

CREATE, PRIORITIZE, AND IMPLEMENT EXPERIENCES

Using the framework of the Touchpoint Experience Wheel, begin to explore points of interactions with customers as well as experiences that can be delivered. Below are the steps to building and using a Touchpoint Experience Wheel to create valuable experiences.

STEP ONE: CREATE THE TOUCHPOINT FRAMEWORK

- **Choose your most important customer.** Determine which segment of customers you want to focus on first. You can segment customers in a variety of areas: demographic (age, gender, location etc.), psychographic (lifestyle, etc.), or business result (total spent, frequency of purchases, number of purchases, etc.).

- **Identify all potential touchpoints.** Go through each quadrant of the Touchpoint Experience Wheel and document as many touchpoints as possible. Any point of interaction with customers can be considered a touchpoint. Make the list as exhaustive as you can. The more touchpoints, the better. For examples of touchpoints, refer to pages 111 through 114.

- **Choose the high-impact touchpoints.** I call these the "moments of truth." They are the touchpoints that you feel will provide the most bang for your buck with respect to influencing

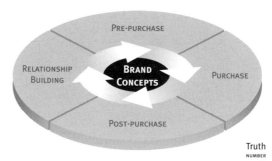

the customer. High-impact touchpoints should be the ones that provide the greatest opportunity to create and deliver experiences. Be careful not to choose too many in the pre-purchase quadrant. Force yourself and your team to zero in on the purchase and post-purchase touchpoints that may not typically be highly interactive, but could be with a little creativity and innovation.

- **Match brand concepts to touchpoints.** Now that you've chosen the high-impact touchpoints, determine which of your brand concepts should be the "drivers" of the experience at each touchpoint. Choose the two most compelling brand concepts based on what you believe are the needs and wants of the customer. Again, be sure to reference the insights gathered from the employee and customer brand image assessments.

STEP TWO: INNOVATE EXPERIENCES

Using the chosen brand concept(s) as stimulus, you can now begin to frame questions that will help you and your team begin thinking about potential experiences. If you have participated in structured brainstorming activities before, you may be familiar with the idea of problem questions such as "How might we …?" or "In what ways can we …?" In this step of the process, you will formulate very similar questions. I call them opportunity questions, as opposed to problem questions.

An important point: When formulating your opportunity questions to position you and your team to innovate experiences, you will want to reference the operational definitions you created for the relevant brand concept. For instance, let's say your company is a jewelry store and one of your brand concepts is Amazing Customer Service. Let's assume that some of the beliefs behind this concept are:

Truth
NUMBER
6
Behaviors and
Experiences
Make the
Invisible
Visible

- We believe customers want **expert advice** for finding gifts for the most meaningful moments in their lives.

- We believe customers deserve **genuine and thoughtful service** from store employees.

- We believe customers want a **quick and efficient check-out** process.

- We believe customers want **packaging that thrills** gift recipients and makes gift-givers proud.

All of these beliefs represent the brand concept of Amazing Customer Service for this hypothetical jewelry business.

Now let's assume that one of the high-impact touchpoints is the in-store selection process — the point where a salesperson in the store is not only showing a variety of jewelry products, but is also providing helpful advice. Let's call this touchpoint The Moment of Choice. This is the point where the customer will make his or her final decision on which product, if any, to purchase.

Here are some opportunity questions that would work well for getting people thinking about experiences that demonstrate Amazing Customer Service at The Moment of Choice.

- How might a salesperson deliver expert advice to help a customer choose the perfect gift to meet his/her needs?

- How can a salesperson demonstrate being genuine and thoughtful when interacting with customers?

To build experiences, break participants into small teams or allow individuals to work independently as they brainstorm ideas for each opportunity question. Then come together, share results, and build off of one another's ideas. Finally, begin to craft the most meaningful, relevant, and actionable experiences for your high-impact touchpoints. You will most likely generate a lot of ideas and, when starting off, the more the better. Remember, it's brainstorming. Don't shoot down other people's ideas. I've never had a client who did not have at least one member on the team who tried to kill a good idea. Don't let it happen. At this point, treat all ideas as viable. Even the craziest ideas can become your best opportunities with a little more creativity and insight.

I recommend hiring a skilled facilitator to guide you and your team through the above innovation steps. Over time, this process will become second nature to your participants and they'll learn to think about the brand concepts at specific touchpoints, ultimately creating experiences that drive productivity of employees, loyalty of customers, and more sales than ever before!

Truth
NUMBER

6

Behaviors and Experiences Make the Invisible Visible

Step Three: Prioritize experiences based on impacts to productivity, loyalty, and sales

At this point, you probably have many more experience ideas than you could ever implement in the next 12 months (or maybe 12 years). You now need an objective way to prioritize each experience so you can know where to invest your time, energy, and financial resources. When prioritizing experiences, ask yourself these questions:

Key result criteria

- Will the experience increase productivity of our employees? If so, by how much?

- Will the experience increase loyalty with our customers? How so?

- Will the experience lead to increased sales opportunities? Are they short-term? Long-term?

Productivity
Loyalty
+ Sales
_____
Key Results

POSITIVE IMPACT CRITERIA

• How much will customers value the experience?

• Will the experience positively influence perceptions with respect to our brand concepts?

NEGATIVE IMPACT CRITERIA

• Will the experience require a large financial investment?

• Will the experience require a large human capital investment (people time)?

• Will the experience slow down other important initiatives?

Go to www.brandintegrity.com/truth6 to download an Experience Prioritization Template that has the most notable criteria to consider.

STEP FOUR: IMPLEMENT EXPERIENCES AND TRACK FOR SUCCESS

The final step in this process requires assigning ownership, accountability, and timing to each of the top chosen experiences. The five keys to success for implementing and tracking experiences are:

1. Assigning ownership for each experience initiative.

2. Determining reasonable timing for implementation of each experience including key milestones to hit along the way toward full implementation.

3. Documenting specific ways to track the success of the experience.

4. Bringing leaders together to share successes and challenges.

5. Communicating progress to company employees regularly throughout the year. Doing so greatly enhances understanding and commitment to the brand strategy.

Now that you understand the Making the Invisible Visible approach for building and operationally defining brand concepts

Truth
NUMBER
6
Behaviors and
Experiences
Make the
Invisible
Visible

and creating experiences, it's time to dive into the human element of brand-building. Hopefully you've recognized that the brand is delivered by people — in this case, your employees. You may be surprised to know that employees are not really your greatest asset.

Read on ...

Truth
NUMBER

6

Behaviors and Experiences Make the Invisible Visible

Truth
NUMBER

Employees Are NOT Your Greatest Asset

....

TOPICS

IDEAS ⋯⋙ ACTION

1 Complete the Experience Scorecard	2 Put On Your Productivity Hat	3 Ensure a Brand Match

7.1 Is Your Brand at Work?

Is your brand at work doing the things it needs to be doing to make your organization more profitable? It's an interesting question that may also seem confusing. Let me shed some light on it. Think of your brand as an employee. An employee comes to work each day and does one of three things with respect to the productivity and profitability of your company:

1. **Performs well, positively impacting productivity and profits.** These are the best kind — your all-stars. Typically about 20 percent of your workforce falls into this category.

2. **Does okay, not really having a positive or negative impact on your productivity or profit goals.** Unfortunately, this group typically represents about half or more of your workforce.

3. **Underperforms, hindering productivity and draining profits.** These are the employees who are either motivated but poorly trained or have simply "quit" while still on the job — and on your payroll. Ouch!

Your brand is no different from an employee. It has personality attributes and associations in the market that influence the minds of your customers. Your brand works to encourage customers to take action. It can lead them to insist on buying and using your product or service. Or, it can lead them to perceive your product or service as okay and easy to trump, causing indifference. That indifference opens the door to your competitors, ultimately forcing you to lower your price and reduce your profit in an attempt to earn their business. This results in underperformance by your company, which in turn leads to budget-wasting advertising and marketing promises and expectations that your company (and the people in it) can't deliver. Worse yet, it can lead customers away — far, far away — from your product or service, leaving little chance of winning them back no matter how much you change or spend.

Therefore, if you have an employee and a customer, then you have a brand to build and manage. View your brand as the most important employee in your company, the one person who, if managed properly, will lead to incredible efficiencies in productivity and dramatic improvements in profitability. The fact is, on a week-to-week, day-to-day, hour-to-hour basis, your company's brand is either helping to grow your business or hindering its progress. Doesn't this seem like something you should be managing? I thought so!

> *If you have an employee and a customer, then you have a brand to build and manage.*

"Hello, Brand!"

7.2 The Good, the Bad, and the Ugly

Employees are not your greatest asset. Anyone who says they are is simply using rhetoric with little thought about the logic behind the statement. Unfortunately, the truth is that, for most companies, the employees are not the greatest asset. If you want a list of companies where employees are considered the greatest asset, visit the annual *Fortune* magazine "100 Best Companies to Work For" article. There you will find companies who believe the rhetoric, act on it, and build performance-based, profitable companies because of it. Companies such as:

Wegmans Food Markets
Philosophy = "We can achieve our goals only if we fulfill the needs of our own people."

The Container Store
Philosophy = "One great person equals three good people."

The right employees who have the passion and knowledge to do the right things at work are your greatest asset.

On the other hand, the wrong people are your company's greatest catastrophe. These are the individuals who should never have been hired in the first place. They have drained training resources and been difficult to work with, leading to decreased morale and lower productivity. In many cases, these poor performers have found ways to directly or indirectly deter customer loyalty all the while exhausting your payroll. Far from an asset.

Your mediocre people are your company's greatest drain on overall resources. These are the ones who end up hanging around the longest. Why? Because many companies operate from the perspective that time and work experience will enhance productivity. Leaders at this kind of company will not come out and say it; they let their actions do the talking. They view training and development of people as an expense, not an investment. They continually pay out bonuses to individuals who simply do not deserve them and stay egregiously loyal to employees who have put in many years of service regardless of their work ethic and, in some cases, the quality of work delivered. Yes, these leaders will sometimes find ways to shift employees to different job functions to "better place" them, only to lower the quality of output within other functional areas. Do you know this type of leader? This wimp, with little to no backbone?

In many cases, the mediocre employee sticks around for years, infesting the work culture with mediocrity and keeping the company from truly achieving its desired success.

Here is a fact to keep in mind. Not all employees are of equal value in the workplace. Seems obvious, doesn't it? Some people build team strength and others drain it. Some people drive results, some prohibit results. If this is the case, why do companies create homogeneous work activities focused on keeping costs down versus developing great people? And why do their unenlightened HR professionals (urgh ... Talent Managers) help them do it? Why is more attention paid to the activities that employees need to perform versus the measurable outcomes of those activities? Why are performance evaluations conducted more to keep companies out of legal trouble and less to truly construct pathways for future development?

Because "all" employees are not *really* the greatest asset!

If your company is like most, you have three classes of employees as they relate to overall company success (productivity, customer loyalty, and sales):

1. The Good: Approximately 20 percent of your employee base.

These are your star performers — the ones who are carrying the weight of all your underachievers. You'll find that these employees consistently:

• Deliver work product in a productive fashion, making others around them look good in the process.

• Enhance the overall customer experience, leading to a more loyal base of customers.

• Position the company to sell more stuff to existing and new customers.

Star Performer

• Pick up the slack for your mediocre and lousy employees and therefore become more and more frustrated in their daily work.

Each day you risk losing these overachieving good employees who have a dramatically positive impact on your company's bottom-line success and desired work culture.

2. The Bad: Approximately 60 percent of your employee base.

These are your mediocre employees — the ones who have been draining your resources year after year. They are doing more harm than good for your company but they probably think they do mostly good. In reality, these mediocre resource-drainers:

- Deliver work product that is sometimes good and sometimes fair but rarely great, decreasing your ability to truly delight customers.

Mediocre Performer

- Provide some customer experiences that are enhanced, leading to loyalty. But some are not. These individuals tend to shine for some customers and not for others, risking damage to the overall brand image of your company due to the lack of consistency that customers desire.

- Rarely have a significant impact on bottom-line sales results.

- Often want to be good employees but just don't know how.

The last bullet above is good news! Your company can shrink the percentage of Bad (60%) and beef up the Good (20%) by defining what superior performance looks like. If you want it, you must define it.

3. The Ugly: Approximately 20 percent of your employee base.

These are your poor performers — the ones who are responsible for underachieving and dragging down the morale of your star performers. These employees are absorbing your payroll and spreading their negative energy across your company like a cancer. You'll find these employees consistently:

- Deliver work product that does not meet minimum standards.

- Diminish the overall customer experience, leading to lower customer loyalty and even fewer referrals.

BRAND CHALLENGE

"Complacency among some of our employees is really starting to weigh down our best performers."

- Position the company to lose sales opportunities to existing and prospective customers.

- Frustrate your Good employees who are working overtime to pick up their slack.

Poor Performer

What should you do about these people? Fire them. You won't regret it. Many of them have quit on your company already. That's right, they've quit already. They come to work each day weighing your company down and taking from its payroll while reducing productivity, loyalty, and sales.

This sounds harsh, I know. But, if you don't find a way to either develop them or fire them, you will continue to lose the respect of the best because you don't deal effectively with the worst.

You will lose the respect of the best when you don't deal effectively with the worst.

Up to this point, I have written this chapter assuming that your company is typical. You might dispute the percentages I've estimated for each employee type, but can you really dispute the categorical framework? Do you really believe that you can't bucket your employees into the Good, the Bad, and the Ugly?

My fundamental belief is that leaders of great companies cannot afford to take a casual approach to mediocrity. They simply cannot put up with it. They — you — need to break through it.

A brand strategy can help leaders do just that. A brand strategy that over time will paint a prettier picture of your Good, Bad, and Ugly includes an Employer Brand component. Build it and they will come (sorry for the hackneyed expression, but it works).

Truth
NUMBER
7
Employees
Are NOT Your
Greatest Asset

SOLUTION

"Train them or fire them! Start believing and behaving as if training and development is an investment in your people, not an expense to the company."

7.3 Building the Employer Brand

If you want employees to be your greatest asset, then make them the central figure of your brand-building efforts. Don't brand for the neighborhood by dressing up the outside of your house while leaving the inside unattended as a haven for your Bad and Ugly employees to drive down productivity, ruin the work culture, and provide disservice to customers.

The Employer Brand is made up of the meaningful expectations (people, processes, values, and behaviors) that your company is known for as an employer because of the experiences and opportunities provided to employees. The experiences provided to employees shape the work culture. They begin from the day an employee candidate meets a prospective employer. A strong Employer Brand will lead your company to the ultimate goal of gaining employee commitment.

A company focused on building an Employer Brand thinks hard about choosing the right people for the right jobs. It outlines what success looks like for the job not only today, but also for the future. A strong focus is also applied to finding the kind of people to perform in those jobs. Doing so ensures that these companies will hire, promote, and develop the best candidates.

How could you *not* do it this way? As a company, your most reliable resource should be your people. It is one element in business that you can control. Your people drive business results through their judgments, experiences, and capabilities. Success and/or failure is up to them on a daily basis.

THE BIG IDEA

If you spoke with the CEOs of the companies listed on *Fortune's* "100 Best Companies to Work For," you would find that they already know this big idea. That's why their companies make the list. Some of them make the list year after year.

You must first delight the workplace if you want to delight the marketplace.

Why Brand for Employees?

The reason for focusing your brand-building efforts on employees is quite simple — employees have choices! Just like customers, they are attracted to companies with strong brands — companies that stand for something meaningful.

Employees have four choices with respect to achieving desired business results for your company:

1. **Join:** "I choose to join your company, do great work, and help achieve goals and objectives."

2. **Stay:** "I choose to stay with your company, becoming a valuable employee over time."

3. **Grow:** "I choose to develop my skills and capabilities, becoming more valuable to your company over time."

4. **Contribute:** "I choose to consistently deliver and make a positive impact on bottom-line success."

Expected Results of Building the Employer Brand

Building an Employer Brand enhances the power of the positive. Said another way, it increases the upbeat energy in your company and propels employees, work teams, and leaders to accomplish remarkable results.

Having a company brand strategy and subsequent brand that employees find to be meaningful and relevant leads to:

- **Passion and sponsorship:** The right employees, motivated by the same desirable outcomes, willingly head in the same direction as the company and as one another.

- **A positive work culture:** Internal excitement is focused on embracing change, not fighting it.

- **Employee commitment:** Employees understand how they fit into and have an impact on the company.

- **Customer loyalty:** Because experiences are meaningful and stimulate incredible loyalty. This happens only when employees understand the benefits customers are looking for and the

Truth
NUMBER

7

Employees
Are NOT Your
Greatest Asset

133

uniqueness with which your company can deliver those benefits. This allows employees to connect emotionally with the brand, optimizing their ability to delight customers.

7.4 Talent Management: The Hidden Value of HR

Is your human resource department focused on managing your people's talent? Where do your HR leaders spend their time? On administrative functions and cost-reducing activities or on improving the quality of the people in your organization?

Since the right people doing the right things are the greatest asset to a company, one would hope that an internal strategic function would take charge of developing this asset. This could be viewed as a charge for human resources. Or not.

In his article, "Why We Hate HR," Keith Hammonds claims that "HR people are, for most practical purposes, neither strategic nor leaders."

Hammonds further brings to light the point that, "The human resources trade long ago proved itself, at best, a necessary evil — and at worst, a dark bureaucratic force that blindly enforces nonsensical rules, resists creativity, and impedes constructive change. HR is the corporate function with the greatest potential — the key driver, in theory, of business performance — and also the one that most consistently underdelivers."

Hammonds' article supports his position with results from a 2005 survey by the Hay Group:

• "Forty percent of employees commended their companies for retaining high-quality workers."

• "Forty-one percent agreed that performance evaluations were fair."

• "Fifty-eight percent rated their job as favorable. Most said they had few opportunities for advancement — and that they didn't know, in any case, what was required to move up."

134

The Hay Group study also reported that "about half of workers below the manager level believed their companies took a genuine interest in their well-being."

These statistics are absolutely pathetic. Can you believe this?

About 60 percent of employees feel that performance evaluations are not fair and that their company (the one they get out of bed each day to work for) is really NOT focused on hiring and retaining good workers. What a disgrace! Even if these figures were off by, let's say, 20 percent, this reality is terrible and needs to be dramatically enhanced.

If this doesn't sound like talent management, that's because it isn't! Most leaders recognize that companies with the most talent will win more and lose less. In order to bring winning to reality, human resource personnel should be making the most of their, well, human resources.

> Truth #8: *Gaining Buy-in Is the Only Way to Execute a Brand Strategy* describes an approach to performance management that will engage, inspire, and motivate your workforce to ensure that the scary statistics just provided don't infiltrate your company.

Focusing on maximizing the value of the people in your organization requires a change in mind-set and role accountability. Who in HR will be responsible for administrative functions that protect the company's ass, making sure everyone is playing by the rules? Who will be managing talent, ensuring the company is getting the best and brightest people — the people who will be most productive, delight customers, spark loyalty, and enable the company to deliver top-line sales results? In most businesses, people are the greatest source of competitive advantage. That's why HR needs to be focused on talent management activities such as selecting, evaluating, coaching, recognizing, re-purposing, and terminating.

Hammonds states that human resources should not forfeit long-term value for short-term cost efficiency. If your vice president of human resources reports to your CFO, then HR in your company is clearly headed in the wrong direction. Says one HR executive, "A financial person is concerned with taking money out of the organization. HR should be concerned with putting investments in."

Don't waste the opportunity to truly manage the talent of your company just because you don't have the HR staff to do it. Begin with HR people. Find a leader in HR that seeks the hidden strategic value of human resources — one who recognizes that the only thing worse than developing an employee and having them leave is not developing them and having them stay!

The only thing worse than developing an employee and having them leave is not developing them and having them stay!

FINANCIAL-ONLY VIEW   TALENT & PROFIT VIEW

"Save money, cut costs!"

"Coach our people. Proactively manage our talent, promote the best, and fire the worst."

IDEAS ⋯⋗ ACTION

COMPLETE THE EXPERIENCE SCORECARD

Schedule a meeting with a few leaders in your company. As pre-work to the meeting, have each complete the Experience Scorecard. The scorecard will provide insight into the experience employees have working for your company as well as the experience customers have doing business with your company.

To download an Experience Scorecard, go to www.brandintegrity.com/truth7.

Have each participant complete the scorecard without looking at the points scoring section. In the meeting, gather the scores and insights from each participant. For each statement on the scorecard, document realistic and accurate summaries of your company's strengths and weaknesses. The results of this exercise will not only lead to dynamic, healthy conversations among your fellow leaders, it will also provide clear direction for your future brand strategy efforts. For instance, if on the employee part of the scorecard, leaders on your team scored very low on statement number four ("our employees understand our most important customers and how to delight them with our products and services") then clearly your brand strategy implementation efforts should include extra energy and

The Brand Integrity Experience Scorecard

Employee Scorecard:
How well does your brand deliver experiences that drive employee productivity and loyalty?

Customer Scorecard:
How well does your brand deliver experiences that drive customer loyalty and acquisition?

Rating Scale | Strongly Disagree | 0 | 1 | 2 | Agree | 3 | 4 | 5 | Strongly Agree

Please rate each statement and total your score.

1. Our employees understand our "vision for success" (The big picture) and trust our leadership to get us there

2. Our employees communicate effectively and strive to build a performance-driven work culture

3. Our employees feel comfortable and are willing to refer our products/services to potential customers

4. Our employees understand our most important customers and how to delight them with our products/services

5. Our employees feel good about working for our company and are inspired and motivated to achieve exceptional results

Total Score

Please rate each statement and total your score.

1. Our customers are willing to pay a higher premium for our products/services then for our competitions

2. When people think about our product/service category, our company is one of the ones they think of

3. If our brand disappeared tomorrow, our customers would be very upset and speak out about it

4. If our brand fell victim to bad press, our customers would give us the benefit of the doubt

5. Our customers seek opportunities to advocate about our products/services (refer our products/services to others)

Total Score

| Scoring Key | 21 – 25 An Experience Brand (Amazing Performance) | 16 – 20 Signs of a Brand-Driven Organization (Good Performance) | 11 – 15 An untapped Brand (Below average Performance) | 6 – 10 A Brand in need of help (Poor Performance) | 0 – 5 Call the funeral director |

Brand Integrity, Inc. Brand-Driven Scorecards   60 Park Ave. Rochester, NY 14607   www.brandintegrity.com © 2005 Brand Integrity, Inc.

resources focused on communicating with employees the desired outcomes that are most important to customers in a relationship with your company and its products and services.

Put On Your Productivity Hat

Put on your productivity and profit hat and think for a moment about your workforce. Choose a group of employees and write their names on a piece of paper. Answer the following two questions below each name.

Question 1: Does this employee have a positive attitude about work and demonstrate it with energy and motivation to do a great job? (Rank this employee on a scale of 1 to 10 with 10 being great and 1 being awful.)

Question 2: Is this employee consistently productive in doing a job that enables the company to be more profitable? (Use the same rating scale as in the first question.)

Now plot your chosen employees in the following Attitude and Profitability Grid: Friends, A-Players, Dogs, and Culture Killers.

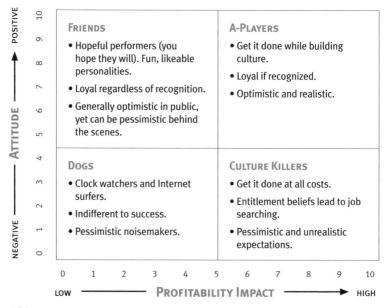

Truth
NUMBER
7
Employees
Are NOT Your
Greatest Asset

Where do your employees fall on the Attitude and Profitability Grid? Consider making this type of ranking and classification a part of your employee evaluation process. Doing so will give managers a unique, effective way to view the talent they are managing. This framework not only helps to classify employees into categories that can motivate employee development initiatives, it also provides managers with a consistent way to view employee success — from the perspective of employee attitudes and the profitability of the company. Better attitudes will drive more consistent desirable behaviors, which in turn will lead to greater profitability. From an employee development perspective, managers can become focused on turning Friends, Dogs, and Culture Killers into A-Players. Now *that* will be a rewarding experience!

ENSURE A BRAND MATCH

Win more and lose less in the hiring game. How? By implementing a Brand Match hiring process that includes the use of a hiring scorecard approach to evaluating and choosing the best possible candidates.

To ensure a Brand Match, you need a process. From prospecting a candidate through the hiring process and into training and orientation, you as a leader must focus as much or more on learning a candidate's brand potential (ability to deliver the behaviors and experiences of your company) as you do on the technical, job-specific tasks.

Hiring is one of the most critical jobs of any leader. If you hire great people (A-Players) you will get better results with less work in less time. If you do not hire A-Players, you (or another top performer) will have to do their work while managing them and trying to hold them accountable. For you to achieve what you and your company are capable of, you must always try to hire A-Players.

What is an A-Player? An A-Player is someone who you consider to be in the top 10 percent of all candidates *within the salary range* for the position you are hiring. These candidates have proven track records for delivering results in their past jobs.

139

Not striving for A-Players can be very costly. Consider the cost of a bad hire. According to Brad Smart and Geoff Smart in their book *TopGrading*, the average cost of mis-hiring an employee can be 15 times base salary. Consider this for a moment: if you mis-hire a $100,000 employee, it is costing you $1.5 million! Now consider how much time and effort you would spend to save $1.5 million. Other estimates of the cost of mis-hires for more junior positions start at one and a half times the yearly salary.

The bottom line: A-Players are worth the energy, effort, and resources put into prospecting, investigating, and attracting them to your company.

The following is a four-step process to follow to increase the likelihood of a Brand Match.

1. **Build an A-Pipeline.** In this step, you ensure that you have a ready supply of exceptional candidates and screen the ones that best fit your company. It is important to note that this process should be happening all of the time regardless of current openings. This step requires constant communications with potential candidates. Networking by you and your peers at work is required!

2. **Investigative Interviewing.** Next you run candidates through a rigorous interview process and a comprehensive reference check. This type of interview process is different (and longer) than most. It focuses on past career successes and failures, followed up with reference checks to verify the information provided. In addition, group interviews should be done with A-Players in the department that the employee will work in or with the people who will report to him/her if they're a manager.

3. **The Offer.** Once you are confident of a Brand Match, provide the candidate a clear offer and convince him or her to say yes. After the interview, you have a very good idea of what the candidate's strengths, weaknesses, and career goals are. When you present the Offer, use these to show how the job you are offering will help the candidate use his/her strengths and achieve his/her career goals. The Offer is an ideal time to further communicate

the Brand Lens concepts that are most important to the candidate's job and to explain why you feel he or she will do a great job delivering the expected results.

4. **Orientation.** This step in the process starts from the moment the Offer is accepted. You need to create experiences that immediately show the candidate that he/she made the right decision. The Orientation process must provide clear indications of what is going to happen and when to impress candidates and get them excited about coming on board. The Orientation should include several touchpoints between the new employee and the Brand Lens concepts.

> In Truth #8: *Gaining Buy-in Is the Only Way to Execute a Brand Strategy,* I will provide direction for developing self-assessments on the brand behaviors an employee should be doing consistently. Sharing this type of assessment would be a great experience for a new employee during Orientation.

Signing the Brand Charter,[1] taking a fun brand quiz, or participating in brand strategy Lunch & Learn activities are other ideas that my clients have found to be quite successful.

The most critical part of the Brand Match process and the most difficult to master is the interviewing step. As you do this step, you will want to keep score using a hiring scorecard that has brand-specific questions tailored to each job position. Doing so will position any manager in your company to be more successful finding the "right" people.

For each brand concept that makes up your overall brand strategy, create a list of questions that when answered by a prospective employee will provide an indication of how that person will fit in the company.

For instance, if you are the hiring manager at a technology store and you are hiring someone to be a sales clerk, you would most likely want

1 Brand Charter: A document that employees sign that sets expectations for delivering the brand behaviors and experiences required to sustain a strong brand image internally and in the market.

someone who knows something about technology. Now suppose one of your company's brand concepts is Leaders in Technology. Suppose there are three candidates and each is asked to describe his or her favorite technology publication or trade association.

Here are some hypothetical responses:

Prospect 1: "I don't have a favorite technology publication, but I love *Sports Illustrated*."

Prospect 2: "Huh?"

Prospect 3: "*Wireless World* is a great magazine and last year I really enjoyed going to the local Information Technology seminar at the conference center.

I realize this is a simple example, but it serves the purpose of illustrating my point: if you ask the right questions, you can uncover a candidate's propensity to deliver your company's brand concepts.

To get started on developing your hiring scorecard, choose the three or four most important brand concepts for the job you are trying to fill. Next, craft three to five questions that will give an indication of the individual's ability to deliver upon the brand. When interviewing, rank each response on a scale of one to five.

1 = Does not meet brand expectations.

2 = Partially meets brand expectations.

3 = Meets brand expectations.

4 = Exceeds brand expectations.

5 = Far exceeds brand expectations.

The initial questions you create and the probing questions you may need to follow up with must serve the purpose of creating a full picture of the candidate as he or she relates to your brand. Once every candidate has been interviewed, you can score each one using the scale above. This approach makes the hiring decision more about the brand and the candidate's ability to deliver it than about personal agenda — gut opinions and assumptions that often lead to bad hiring decisions. The right brand-related questions will enable you to learn more about candidates' past and present accomplishments, ideologies, and passions. You'll learn how they think and what drives their ambitions. Imagine having all of this data and being able to tell more clearly whether a candidate is a good fit with your company and its brand strategy.

Below are a series of hiring questions for a professional service firm, technology company, and retail store. For each set of questions, I provide a sample Brand Lens concept and some questions that would be relevant to the concept. The purpose of this list is to provide a bit more guidance on how to create questions that align with the brand strategy. For a typical job, you would want to have at least three to five questions for each relevant Brand Lens concept.

PROFESSIONAL SERVICE FIRM

• Brand Lens concept: We work in a **Team-based Project Management** environment.

  - Can you share an example where poor project management has strained a work team and/or client relationship?

  - Have you ever worked in a team-based environment? What did you like about working on a team? What did you not like about working on a team?

TECHNOLOGY COMPANY

• Brand Lens concept: We are a **Trusted Partner.**

  - What does the word *trust* mean to you? What do you think the word *trust* means to our customers?

  - What is one of the most unethical activities you have witnessed in your professional career? How did your employer handle it? What did you think about the way it was handled? How would you have handled it differently?

- Brand Lens concept: We strive to be a **Great Place to Work.**
  - What's the best job you've ever had and what made it great?
  - Can you provide an example of a time when you recognized a fellow employee for a job well done?

These sample questions provide some guidance to get you started. Work with your team to create insightful questions for each of your company's Brand Lens concepts. Then plug your questions into our Hiring Scorecard. It's on our Web site. It's free. Go get it.

Truth
NUMBER
7
Employees
Are NOT Your
Greatest Asset

 For a Hiring Scorecard template, go to www.brandintegrity.com/truth7.

Finding/hiring a great employee is critical for success. Providing a performance-based culture is necessary to keeping the best employees. The next Truth will introduce you to a performance program that will ensure you sustain a Brand Match.

Truth

7

Employees
Are NOT Your
Greatest Asset

Truth
NUMBER

Gaining Buy-in Is the Only Way to Execute a Brand Strategy

Truth
NUMBER

8

Gaining Buy-in
Is the Only
Way to Execute
a Brand
Strategy

TOPICS

8.1 What Does It Mean to Achieve Buy-in?

8.2 The Power of Behaviors

8.3 The Pathway to Buy-in

8.4 Mission Statements Suck!

8.5 Striving for a Performance Culture

8.6 Barriers to Buy-in

8.7 Realistic Expectations for Achieving Buy-in

8.8 A Tribute to Behaviors

IDEAS ⋯⋯⋗ ACTION

| 1 Build a Brand-driven Performance System | 2 Close the Performance Gap |

147

Several years ago, IBM launched one of the funniest ad campaigns I've ever seen. Here was the scene: two consultants are sitting in front of a CEO in an incredibly large high rise office overlooking a beautiful metropolitan city.

Truth
NUMBER

8

Gaining Buy-in
Is the Only
Way to Execute
a Brand
Strategy

The commercial begins with the two consultants babbling in consultant speak about strategy development and implementation. After a few moments, the CEO looks both consultants in the eye and says, "Okay, let's do it." The two consultants look at the CEO with a stunned expression. Then they look back at each other. After an uncomfortable pause, Consultant One says, "We don't actually do what we propose." Consultant Two says, "Yeah, we just propose it."

This Dilbert-esque spot is funny stuff because it represents what has become so typical in corporate America. Business leaders invest countless dollars and people hours in developing strategies, only to receive fancy binders that have little effect other than collecting dust in the executive suite. IBM recognized this and was attempting to play off the idea by saying that its consultants will actually implement the strategy, ensuring you see the business results of your consulting project. Thank you Big Blue!

All right, so it is fairly obvious that many companies invest in strategy development and then drop the ball when it comes to actual implementation. A 1999 *Fortune* article reported that 70 to 90 percent of companies fail at implementing their strategy. Have you been guilty of strategy-dropping in your past? Sure you have. The question is, why?

Why do companies fail, time and again, to implement strategies, programs, and initiatives? Whether it's a brand strategy, process improvement program, or customer service initiative, great ideas and initiatives fail resulting in disappointment and wasted budgets. My answer to this question is one of the most important insights you will gain from this book.

Companies fail in implementing strategies because their employees don't buy into them.

148

Truth
NUMBER

8

Gaining Buy-in
Is the Only
Way to Execute
a Brand
Strategy

As explained previously, at Brand Integrity Inc. we call our brand strategy development program *Achieving Brand Integrity*. Our philosophy is that you achieve *Brand Integrity* when your employees and customers know you as who you say you are — when your company has achieved its desired brand image.

No Buy-in = No Achieving Brand Integrity

Brand Integrity cannot be achieved without buy-in from leaders and employees. Your company will never be consistently known for its brand concepts unless leaders and employees are engaged in the beliefs behind each brand concept and motivated to do the behaviors to bring them to life. Neither will happen without buy-in.

So, what is buy-in?

BUY-IN = Understanding x Commitment x Action

Truth
NUMBER

8

Gaining Buy-in
Is the Only
Way to Execute
a Brand
Strategy

An employee in your company has bought into the brand strategy when the three parts of the formula — understanding, commitment, action — are in place. If any one is at zero, then buy-in equals zero. Plain and simple. You do not have buy-in unless all three components are achieved.

Employees must *understand* the brand concepts and the beliefs, benefits, and behaviors required to do them.

Next, employees must be *committed* to doing the brand concepts. Beyond giving lip service in a meeting or at a company event, employees must really believe they can and should hold the same values of the organization and do the behaviors to demonstrate those values.

Finally, employees must actually *do* the brand concepts that are relevant to their role in the company. They must take action! You'll notice I said "relevant to their role." That's because not all brand concepts are relevant to every position in the company. Certain jobs require more focus and attention on specific aspects of the brand simply because of the nature of the work. When reviewing any job category in your company, simply ask yourself, "Which of the brand concepts for our company do the people in this job have the greatest opportunity to do each day?" Your answer to this question will spell out the brand drivers[1] that should be the main focus for creating behaviors that employees should be held accountable to do.

1 Brand drivers are a few selected brand concepts chosen for a job category based on expected impact on success.

WHAT IT MEANS TO UNDERSTAND

To understand a brand concept means an employee can comprehend and embrace it within the context of your company's business environment. If it makes sense to them and they believe in it, then *understanding* has been accomplished.

Total understanding requires that employees become educated and knowledgeable about:

1. **Who you are:** The brand concepts your company aspires to be known for in its marketplace. *Who you are* equals your current brand image plus the desired brand image.

2. **How you do it:** The behaviors and experiences employees do with respect to each brand concept. *How you do it* must deliver *who you are!*

3. **Why it matters:** This can be easy to lose track of in the quest to gain understanding. Ignoring *why* delivering upon the brand concepts is important to target audiences makes the step of *understanding* superficial at best. Superficial understanding of your brand concepts will make it nearly impossible to achieve *commitment*.

Truth
NUMBER
8

Gaining Buy-in
Is the Only
Way to Execute
a Brand
Strategy

WHAT IT MEANS TO COMMIT TO A BRAND CONCEPT

The fact that employees comprehend and believe in a brand concept does not mean they will actually commit to doing it and doing it consistently (beyond lip service).

Commitment to delivering brand-driven behaviors typically requires that employees agree to do something differently from before. They must

"Consistency is king."

change, and change is something that inherently makes people uneasy. That's why it's often the case that employees commit only to find a few weeks later that they are still not putting forth the necessary effort to modify their perspectives (beliefs) and deliver the required behaviors.

The best way to get employees to commit is to provide them an opportunity to contribute and personalize the brand to their role in the company. The Ideas Into Action section at the end of this chapter will get you started.

Commitment to delivering brand-driven behaviors typically requires that employees agree to do something differently from before. They must change.

Someone once said, "The most effective and enjoyable way for most of us to cope with change is to help create it."

WHAT IT MEANS TO TAKE ACTION

Truth
NUMBER

8

Gaining Buy-in
Is the Only
Way to Execute
a Brand
Strategy

Action = doing! You're either doing the required brand-driven behaviors and experiences, or you're not. All the understanding and commitment in the world won't matter a bit if an employee doesn't *do* the strategy. To achieve buy-in, you need to ensure that employees know how to take action and are able to actually do it.

Implementing a brand strategy is about doing, not saying.

8.2 The Power of Behaviors

The power of employees internalizing, personalizing, and taking action to do a brand is remarkable.

> In the grand scheme of your business reality, the behaviors you define for your employees are all that really matter when it comes to doing any strategy. Behaviors are the beliefs of the organization turned into action. They define what a successful brand looks like at the individual employee level.

Most important, having well-articulated and documented brand behaviors enables company leadership to infuse accountability into the workforce. Since you can clearly see someone doing a behavior, you can easily set expectations and enforce accountability.

John Kotter, a Harvard business professor and world-renowned expert on organizational change management, makes the following point, "The central issue is never strategy, structure, culture, or systems. . . . The core of the matter is always about changing the behavior of people."

Of course it's difficult to change behaviors. That's why so many companies fail to achieve buy-in to their strategies. In most cases, the leaders and their staff don't even know what the desired behaviors are. This is why the Making the Invisible Visible brand strategy development approach is so valuable. It is a proven approach for bringing leaders together to define who they are *and* what the required behaviors are to *do* it.

If you as a leader in your company are not willing to define what success looks like behaviorally, then don't expect employees to deliver it. Expect them to determine their own behaviors based on their own belief systems.

Stephen Covey, author of *The 7 Habits of Highly Successful People* (one of the best-selling books of all time), understands what makes people, and companies, successful. In 2004, Covey published *The 8th Habit*. In this book, buried on page 227, Covey highlights one of the most insightful challenges in our business world today. If you have the book, go directly to this page. If you don't have the book, and you want a much longer read than this book, I recommend you buy it.

Covey claims, "One of the greatest challenges that business leaders encounter is that of working to cascade and TRANSLATE the corporate vision from 30,000 feet into actionable line-of-sight behaviors among front-line workers to achieve critical objectives."

Think about this quote for a minute. Really, put down the book for a moment and ponder Covey's quote. Now look back at the Making the Invisible Visible model in Truth #6.

You will notice that this model solves exactly what Covey is pointing out. Defining the brand is not the end of your work. You must translate the strategy into line-of-sight behaviors, make them personal to employees, and get those employees to buy into doing them. The Ideas Into Action section of this chapter provides direction on how to accomplish the all-important task of personalizing behaviors to each job category to ensure total buy-in.

Helping employees understand what on-brand behaviors look like enables them to modify their beliefs, adapt their attitudes, and change their behaviors. Here comes an insightful thought:

The Brand Lens you build should be a picture of your company's future with your employees in it!

Truth
NUMBER

8

Gaining Buy-in
Is the Only
Way to Execute
a Brand
Strategy

Making the brand personal to each employee requires they see the big picture of their impact on:

- **Their own success.** Don't assume employees will make a logical connection between delivering a brand concept and the benefit from doing so. In most cases, they won't. As a company leader, you need to make that connection visible for them.

- **Company success.** Don't assume employees understand how they make a difference in the grand scheme of the company's success. Most companies overlook the importance of educating employees on the big picture of success.

Help your employees see the importance of the brand strategy and work will take on new meaning for them. It will become personal!

BRAND CHALLENGE

"Sometimes we struggle to get employees to be passionate about the success of our company."

8.3 The Pathway to Buy-in

Employees will pass through a series of phases in their pathway to understanding, committing to, and taking action on your brand strategy. Each step in the pathway is critical to ensuring that buy-in is achieved.

EMPLOYEE PATHWAY TO BUY-IN

1. **Denial.** The denial stage results from a lack of understanding about the business reality and branding as a viable strategy.

   - Employees think: "I don't understand what we're trying to accomplish. This brand strategy is a flavor of the month. Stop wasting my time so that I can get my work done today. Or tomorrow. Or whenever I get to it since I define what success looks like because you have not."

2. **Resistance.** This is caused by strong beliefs about obstacles that will prohibit successful execution of the brand strategy.

   - Employees think: "Our company doesn't have the right people or operational processes in place to really do the brand strategy — we won't be able to keep the promises our leaders want to make."

   - "Since we're doomed to fail because of the people we have, this branding initiative will only increase my workload. Ugh!"

3. **Exploration.** This signals a desire to learn more.

   - Employees think: "Okay, the company might be onto something meaningful after all. What can I do to bring the brand to reality?"

4. **Commitment.** This is generated from the belief that change is desirable.

   - Employees think: "Leadership seems pretty committed to this. They're still talking about it. Wow! This might not be a flavor of the month after all. The leaders seem to be aligned around this cause."

Truth
NUMBER

8

Gaining Buy-in Is the Only Way to Execute a Brand Strategy

SOLUTION

"Help them see and understand the direct impact they have in contributing to the company's success. Make it clear. Make it visible."

Leaders must be careful not to try to take employees from denial straight to commitment. The steps of resistance and exploration are important in helping employees make the brand personal and create meaning out of the brand-building process.

In helping employees down the pathway of buy-in, it's important to acknowledge that "Rah Rah" kickoff events, T-shirts, mouse pads, and posters won't be nearly enough. It will take more than a motivational speech or a training class to ensure that employees understand the power your brand can have in stimulating cultural transformation and business results.

Truth
NUMBER

8

Gaining Buy-in
Is the Only
Way to Execute
a Brand
Strategy

8.4 Mission Statements Suck!

The dreaded mission statement. It seems as if every company has one and yet nobody knows what it is or what it really means.

Got a company mission statement? Of course you do! If you walked through the office and asked employees to recite two words of it, would they be able to? Of course not! Why? Because it is meaningless to them. They had nothing to do with creating it and they don't see how it applies to them. The reason they can't connect with it is that it doesn't connect to them.

I actually worked with a CEO who would stop employees impromptu in the hall and ask them to recite the mission. If they did it successfully, he would give them $20. This became old after a while. Some took the time to memorize the mission, but most didn't even bother. Those who did take the time to memorize it still found it meaningless. Mission accomplished? I think not!

Mission statements are often meaningless because they are not operationalized. Therefore very few, if any, employees actually know how to do the mission. Nice to know what it is. Much better to be able to do it.

Coming up with the mission statement is simple. There is a book by Jeffrey Abrahams called *The Mission Statement Book: 301 Corporate Mission Statements From America's Top Companies*. This book will cover all you need to know about mission statements. It has 400-plus pages of examples and insights. Reading it and

drafting your company's mission will be easy. Getting your
employees to buy into it and actually do it will be
quite challenging.

*Mission statements are meaningless
if they are not operationalized.*

THE TWO PRINCIPLES OF BUY-IN

Company events, posters, tchotchkes, and T-shirts won't spearhead
the buy-in process for employees. I'll get to how to do it in a
moment. But first it's important to understand the two leading
principles required to set the stage for the buy-in process:

1. **Expectation clarity:** Leadership must explain up front what
   the standard will be for executing the brand strategy. This
   includes clearly communicating how employees will be judged
   (evaluated), what the penalties for failure will look like, and the
   targets and milestones.

2. **Engagement in the process:** Leadership must involve employees
   in the strategic decisions that involve them by asking for their
   input and allowing them to refute the merits of one another's
   ideas and assumptions. In the case of the brand strategy,
   employees must be asked their opinions about the behaviors that
   should be done in their jobs. Involving employees demonstrates
   respect for them and their ideas. In addition, involving
   employees ensures you get the collective wisdom from those who
   are actually on the front lines doing the work — the individuals
   who know the job best.

Keep these two principles in mind as you read the next section
— the one that answers the question, "What can we do to get
employees to buy into the company's brand strategy?"

THREE WAYS TO BUILD AND SUSTAIN BUY-IN

There are three specific ways to get employees to buy into the
brand strategy. For the record, internal marketing communications
is not one of them. I have purposely left that out. Not because

Truth
NUMBER

8

Gaining Buy-in
Is the Only
Way to Execute
a Brand
Strategy

I don't think communicating with employees is important, but because I'm confident that you've tried it in the past and have found that employees don't pay attention. Marketing communications can wait. Marketing to employees through internal newsletters, brochures, and company events will have its place after you successfully execute the following three approaches to ensuring buy-in. I guarantee 100 percent that, over time (12 to 36 months), if you show some guts and stick to these approaches, you will have achieved buy-in.

1. Integrate the brand strategy into performance management systems by documenting and measuring Brand Competencies™[2] and brand-driven behaviors.

2. Recognize and reward individuals who witness and do "on-brand" behaviors. Put a system in place for recognizing all employees and rewarding some employees.

3. Celebrate successes and share failures with the entire organization.

Question: Who is responsible for defining what successful performance looks like?

Answer: Individuals who hold leadership positions in the company.

2 Brand Competencies are the knowledge, skills, and abilities that describe how an employee can have the most impact on delivering superior on-brand performance, which enhances success in achieving the company's goals and objectives.

It is leadership's responsibility to guide the definition of what successful performance looks like for each job in the company. I use the word "guide" because, to ensure buy-in, you must follow the principles of Expectation clarity and Engagement. Leaders should guide the process but not dominate it. If employees don't feel that they have a say, they won't buy in. Remember, it's critical to engage them in the process.

The following pages provide greater depth on each of the three ways to build and sustain buy-in.

1. Integrate the brand strategy into the performance system.

Integrating the brand strategy concepts into performance systems ensures that all employees know what is expected of them. If you want employees to do the brand strategy, you must allow them to go through the process of knowing what it looks like.

Step 1: Determine the brand drivers for the job category.

Step 2: Create a list of Brand Competencies and associated behaviors that are "must-haves" for employees in the job.

Step 3: Work with two or three of the best performers in the job category to gain more specific input.

Step 4: Bring as many job category employees together as you can to review the Brand Competencies and associated brand-driven behaviors, and allow them the opportunity to make modifications and enhancements.

Truth
NUMBER

8

Gaining Buy-in
Is the Only
Way to Execute
a Brand
Strategy

 To learn more of the details about how to build Brand Competencies and behaviors, go to www.brandintegrity.com/truth8. There you will find the framework for a program enabling the development of proprietary competencies and behaviors. Take a look. I promise you won't be disappointed. Especially compared to your alternatives, which are generic, customer-focused, industry-standard, non-proprietary, "me too" materials that your competition is trying to incorporate into their performance systems!

Building the brand concepts into performance expectations provides an opportunity to define what success looks like (for employees and your company) and to set realistic benchmarks for accountability; benchmarks your employees will actually want to be held accountable for. Imagine employees up, down, and across the organization seeking accountability. It can happen with the right performance system in place. I've seen it.

Integrating your brand into performance expectations also encourages leaders to expose and confront poor performers. These are the individuals who ultimately hinder the productivity of high performers.

Finally, involving employees in the process and using the brand strategy and leadership as guides will inspire and motivate them to learn what it will take to become a great performer. Once they know it, they will try much harder to be it!

Truth
NUMBER

8

Gaining Buy-in
Is the Only
Way to Execute
a Brand
Strategy

Bottom line: Good employees will try hard to meet performance objectives if they know and buy into what good performance is!

2. Recognize and reward individuals who witness and do on-brand behaviors.

You'll notice the word "recognize" comes before "reward." This was done by design because this approach to building and sustaining buy-in begins with the simple act of recognizing others.

> Truth #9: *Most Companies Suck at Capturing Successes and Recognizing People* will take you on a journey of changing your current work culture by implementing a sustainable and profitable recognition and reward program.

For the purpose of explaining recognition's role in ensuring buy-in, it is important to note that most organizations reward employees, but don't truly recognize them effectively. This approach lowers productivity and leads to diminished overall performance.

In addition, it is quite typical to have a situation where only a few individuals — the A-Players — ever get recognized and rewarded, leaving out the majority of your workforce who might eventually become the Dogs. (Refer back to the Attitude and Profitability Grid on page 138.)

The key to brand strategy success is to recognize not just the individuals who *do* on-brand behaviors (Brand Stewards) and deliver experiences. To reinforce understanding, commitment, and action with respect to your brand strategy, you must also recognize and reward the Witnesses — the employees who catch others delivering the brand experience.

Witnesses are actually more important than Brand Stewards. I'll explain more in Truth #9.

3. Celebrate successes and share failures with the entire organization.

If performance expectations are integrated into employee job profiles, job descriptions, and/or performance evaluations of some type and you've put in place a program for catching people delivering the brand behaviors and experiences, then now is the time to celebrate successes.

Sharing examples of success (employees "living the brand") is 10 times more powerful than launching an internal marketing campaign. Nothing beats real-life examples of your employees in action doing the brand strategy. Now do you see why I left internal marketing off the list of the top three ways to build and sustain buy-in?

Again, look to Truth #9 to provide more details on how to celebrate successes to ensure greater buy-in.

> *Bottom line: If your company has the guts and discipline to take on the three initiatives outlined, you will achieve buy-in.*

8.5 Striving for a Performance Culture

The three ways to build and sustain buy-in will engage, inspire, and motivate your employees. If an employee does not become engaged, then he or she may not belong in your company. If this statement makes you a little uneasy, skip ahead for a moment and read the Ideas Into Action section on Closing the Performance Gap. It's at the end of this chapter. If you jump ahead, please make sure you come back.

Truth
NUMBER

Gaining Buy-in
Is the Only
Way to Execute
a Brand
Strategy

Truth
NUMBER

8

Gaining Buy-in
Is the Only
Way to Execute
a Brand
Strategy

Do you want employees who come in, punch the clock (literally or figuratively), go through the tactical motions to get the job done, and then punch out? Of course you don't. What leader would?

You want employees who actually care about the success of the company. This happens when they buy into the strategy. When they know what the strategy means to the company and to them personally. When they know how to do the behaviors and experiences in the strategy. And when they understand why it's important to the company and to customers. When this happens, you will have achieved a brand-driven performance culture.

Remember John Kotter's quote mentioned earlier: "The central issue is never strategy, structure, culture, or systems.… The core of the matter is always about changing the behavior of people."

Think about your employee base as a computer. I know this may sound kind of crazy after just getting down from my soap box about making it personal and engaging employees to participate in defining success. But just for a moment think about the employee base as one big computer. An IBM mainframe! Do you remember those? Okay, just think about the computer on your desk. There are two main components to making the computer perform: hardware and software.

Your company has the same two components. Hardware is equal to the strategy and structure of the company. Software is composed of the beliefs and behaviors of the people in the company.

BRAND CHALLENGE

"We keep losing good employees because they're offered more money by our competition."

If you don't have software on your computer, how useful is it? It simply won't perform to its potential.

If the beliefs and behaviors of your employees don't fit inside the structure of your brand, your company will not achieve optimum performance.

Bottom line: No definition for beliefs and behaviors =
No performance culture.

THE END RESULT: PERFORMANCE MIND-SET AND PERFORMANCE CULTURE

From the perspective of an employee, a performance mind-set means: "I understand my role in the company and the impact I have each day on the success of the company."

Truth
NUMBER
8

Gaining Buy-in
Is the Only
Way to Execute
a Brand
Strategy

From the perspective of the company as a whole, a performance culture means employee behaviors are delivered consistently, which produces desired results in productivity and customer loyalty, and generates new sales opportunities.

"Consistency is king."

Neither a performance mind-set nor the resulting performance culture can be accomplished without the right leadership in place. Leaders are ultimately responsible for defining what success look like and leading others by example. That's why we call them leaders, right?

LEADERSHIP'S ROLE IN MAKING BUY-IN A REALITY

The successful implementation of a brand strategy that will drive culture transformation and positively impact the three key result areas (productivity, loyalty, and sales) have the following three components:

1. Brand Lens concepts that clearly define values, behaviors, and a vision for success.

2. Energy and commitment from leadership who are responsible for championing the brand strategy and leading the charge for buy-in.

3. A comprehensive and actionable approach to implementing the brand strategy. At a minimum, this includes integrating the brand into job descriptions and performance evaluation practices.

SOLUTION

"They're not leaving because of the money! They're leaving because they don't feel they're thriving in your work culture. Begin to build a performance culture and your star performers will stay with you longer!"

The second component, energy and commitment from leadership, is absolutely essential. What good are the Brand Lens concepts if leaders don't buy in, champion them, and build excitement to encourage others to follow?

Leadership must be unified in the development of the Brand Lens concepts that define the desired future state of the company. Don't expect employees to be aligned without alignment among leadership.

Truth

NUMBER

8

Gaining Buy-in
Is the Only
Way to Execute
a Brand
Strategy

Essential characteristics of effective brand-building leaders include: strong beliefs in the Brand Lens concepts, an ability to communicate those beliefs as part of a compelling vision for success, and the courage and energy to manage a culture transformation.

Leadership needs *courage* to:

- Confront all levels of the organization with the business reality in order to help others understand the need for change.
- Reallocate resources to fuel the implementation of the brand strategy.
- Make difficult decisions to keep the brand-building momentum alive. In many cases, these are people-related decisions that are in the best interest of the company. It takes courage to make them.

Leadership needs *energy* to:

- Raise the expectations for performance and accountability. Leaders will need to demonstrate consistent focus on aligning the brand strategy and associated behaviors with individual job category behaviors. This energy starts at the top and permeates throughout the organization, infusing accountability in carrying out the necessary performance evaluations and assessments. Keep in mind that people respect what you inspect. Have the courage, energy, and focus to consistently inspect!

"Consistency
is king."

People respect what you inspect.

- Recognize and reward employees who model the required behaviors and deliver the desired brand experiences. Again, leaders must keep the energy level up and stay focused on the art of finding successes in others and sharing them throughout the company.

Truth
NUMBER

8

Gaining Buy-in
Is the Only
Way to Execute
a Brand
Strategy

IDEAL CONDITIONS FOR ACHIEVING BUY-IN

As with all major initiatives, implementing a brand strategy comes down to a company's willingness to change. How do you know whether the company is ready to engage leaders and employees in a brand-building effort? It depends on what's going on inside the company.

Below is an *incomplete* list of ideal conditions for launching a brand strategy development and implementation initiative:

- New leadership has taken the reins.

- The company is going to or has merged with another organization.

- A new product or service opportunity has opened the door to new markets.

- The competitive landscape has changed and the company must modify business practices or risk being left behind.

- The company needs more inspiration and greater motivation from leaders and employees.

In addition to company readiness, the necessary resources must be available. Both human and financial capital are required to create and implement the brand strategy. Not only must you have enough of the right people on the leadership team, you must also have financial resources to commit to the initiative.

The following matrix provides a framework for estimating your company's readiness and resources for investing in a brand strategy initiative.

Quadrant A

The energy level and motivation to create a strategy are high yet resources are low. Companies in this situation will most likely

165

waste time and money. Initiatives get started but not properly funded. The initiative either stalls completely or is done at half speed/effort.

Quadrant B

With resources and readiness both at high levels, this is the ideal place to be when kick-starting a brand strategy initiative.

Quadrant C

The resources are available but the company doesn't seem to be ready. There could be a lot of reasons the company isn't ready. However, given the importance of the strategic thinking and impact on company performance from creating and implementing a brand strategy, careful consideration should be given to the decision to put off the work. In most cases, if you as the leader stay focused on the implementation of the strategy, then the readiness can be increased as others begin to see the high priority of the initiative. Once the perceived priority level increases, the readiness level magically tends to increase.

Quadrant D

If resources and readiness are both low, you're out of luck. Developing a brand strategy should not be considered at this time. In fact, the challenges in your business are probably so great that you are considering whether being in business is really a logical future step for you and your team.

	A Beware of wasting time and money.	B Highest probability of driving bottom-line success.
HIGH →		
READINESS		
LOW	D Do not consider.	C Extreme focus on implementing is required.

LOW ——— RESOURCES ———→ HIGH

Keep in mind that it's more expensive to implement the brand strategy than it is to create it. If you don't have the resources to implement, don't even start. Just bringing a team of people together to create a strategy will not deliver true value for your company. Instead it will lead to a flavor-of-the-month experience for your team and will diminish your credibility.

8.6 Barriers to Buy-in

I would be remiss if I didn't highlight the barriers to gaining buy-in. It is important to strongly consider your potential barriers. Ignoring barriers that really do exist only leads to wasted efforts and frustrations for all employees. Not recognizing the barriers may set you up for failure! Be honest in exploring them.

Truth
NUMBER

8

Gaining Buy-in
Is the Only
Way to Execute
a Brand
Strategy

One obvious barrier is poor leadership. Without strong leadership at the top of the company, there is little to no chance of achieving buy-in. Implementing a brand strategy is a top-down initiative!

Assuming your company is over the initial hurdle of having a strong leader at the top, the following five barriers to building and implementing a brand strategy should be closely considered, analyzed, and acted upon:

1. **Limited consciousness:** A general lack of awareness by other leaders for the need of a brand strategy. This is typically due to unrealistic views of the current business realities such as a strong belief in the status quo and/or a feeling that things are okay as is without having an eye on what the future might bring. This drives limited knowledge of the true needs of the company.

2. **Low readiness:** The organization doesn't have the right people to develop the strategy, and/or the timing may not be right due to unique aspects of your business cycle or market.

3. **Limited resources:** The need to reprioritize energy, commitment, and focus of leaders and employees. Leaders are required (but often hesitant) to reallocate both people and budgets despite the opportunity to make a smart investment in the growth of the company. Shuffling resources tends to negatively impact the

initiatives of others. As hidden agendas appear, they can kill a brand strategy initiative.

Truth

NUMBER

8

Gaining Buy-in
Is the Only
Way to Execute
a Brand
Strategy

4. Skeptical motivation: The doubt that this will really happen and the subsequent apathy. Leaders must engage and inspire employees to embrace the brand strategy, adopt the beliefs, and deliver those beliefs through attitudes and behaviors. This is easier said than done. If your company has been known for flavor-of-the-month-type activities and initiatives, this barrier becomes much greater because believability in management's "stick-to-itiveness" is questioned.

5. Powerful egos: Internal politics caused by individuals whose beliefs are not aligned with the company or who feel threatened by the brand strategy. This is the largest of all the barriers and the most difficult to overcome. In particular, watch out for the leader who shares the desire to commit to the strategy but never really plans to take action, hoping instead that management will lack the credibility and initiative to stick to the implementation and hold him accountable.

When I began formulating the structure of this book, I paid a visit to Jack Trout, a well-respected author and expert on the subject of brand positioning. Trout coined the term "positioning" as we know it in the business world today. Trout remains a sought-after speaker and consultant, having now written many books on the subject of marketing, positioning, and branding.

Trout was very intrigued with the *Achieve Brand Integrity* book for one reason — the concept of gaining buy-in.

I asked Trout to share with me his thoughts on implementation: "Jack, how many of your clients actually implement the strategies that you create for them?" Having worked with so many clients, he wasn't likely to give me a specific answer and, of course, he didn't.

Trout said, "The majority of my clients are challenged to implement for one reason — egos! If you can find a way to overcome the egotism inside a company, then you really have something special."

168

Well, Brand Integrity Inc. has something special. It's a process called *Achieving Buy-in*. It works! If you stay committed to the principles of clearly set expectations and employee participation, over time egos get put aside and powerful brand alignment becomes a reality.

8.7 Realistic Expectations for Achieving Buy-in

If your barriers are surmountable, you're on your way down the pathway of gaining buy-in: educating employees to secure their understanding, ensuring they are committed to the strategy by personalizing it for them, and tracking the actions (behaviors) employees take to do the strategy.

Realistically, how long should this take? What does that pathway look like for the next one to three years?

Each part of the Buy-in Formula (Understanding, Commitment, and Ability to Take Action) represents a stage in the process.

STAGE 1: SUPERFICIAL (UNDERSTANDING)

In the superficial stage, a lot of awareness is generated about the fact that something is going on. Initial communications and rumors throughout the company have stirred up conversations about potential flavor-of-the-month activity. The calls for "not another high-priority program" can be heard behind the scenes. The brand strategy is rightfully superficial until proven otherwise by management's commitment and action.

STAGE 2: CONCEPTUAL (COMMITMENT)

In the conceptual stage the brand concepts are now being personalized by each employee. This is where initial buy-in begins to take shape. By this stage, the brand concepts are integrated into job descriptions, performance expectations, and evaluation practices. A recognition program may be in place and employees are seeing management's commitment to capturing and recognizing successful on-brand behaviors and achievements. For those employees who are struggling to buy in, this is the stage where they are getting ready to take action ("Hey, this could be

Truth
NUMBER
8

Gaining Buy-in
Is the Only
Way to Execute
a Brand
Strategy

169

really cool") or realizing that their time working for the company may be short-lived ("I can't take any more management bullshit").

STAGE 3: EMOTIONAL (TAKING ACTION)

Truth
NUMBER

8

Gaining Buy-in
Is the Only
Way to Execute
a Brand
Strategy

The emotional stage marks the phase where employees' comfort levels reach an all-time high. Employees feel good about their role in the company and how they make a difference by doing the brand behaviors and experiences. They have personalized the experiences and behaviors for their role in the company. They feel comfortable talking about the company and its unique point of difference in the market. For many, this stage leads to the ultimate goal of passionate advocacy; your employees become true ambassadors for the brand, driving more business through positive attitudes and referrals to their personal networks.

REALISTIC EXPECTATION FOR EMPLOYEE BUY-IN

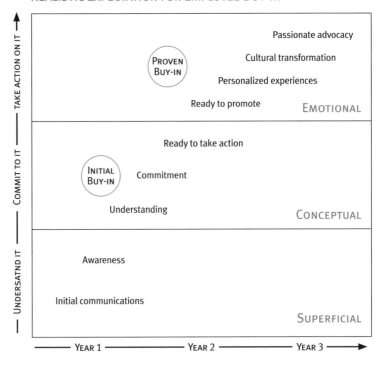

8.8 A Tribute to Behaviors

Up to this point, there has been a lot of information about brand behaviors. They are the beliefs about the Brand Lens concepts, turned into action. They power the experiences that delight employees and customers. Behaviors are observable and measurable and can be personalized right down to the job level. Here are a few final thoughts with respect to the value of the behaviors created in a brand strategy.

Truth
NUMBER

Gaining Buy-in
Is the Only
Way to Execute
a Brand
Strategy

Behaviors can be challenging to create and even more difficult to implement. They require an entirely new perspective on workforce strategies for both managers and human resource professionals. A brand strategy and the associated brand behaviors are not something you can copy from an industry leader. They are established through the foundation of your leadership's beliefs about each Brand Lens concept.

Once you have the strategy and associated behaviors, you can leverage them in your marketing and only then are they believable. Southwest Airlines is a perfect example of this. Recently I boarded a flight on Southwest and was greeted on the plane by a poster outside the cabin that read:

"Providing a service that no other shipper can offer:
OUR PEOPLE!"

Southwest recognizes that its people and the processes and behavioral ways that they've been trained on are proprietary to the company. The behaviors are personal, and it shows. Employees are passionate about them. A few others in the airline industry have been able to replicate similar brand strategies; most have not. JetBlue is another example of a company that has successfully developed a brand strategy and designed the necessary experiences for employees to profitably bring the strategy to life.

Let me share with you a recent, yet very typical, experience designed into the workforce at JetBlue. Aside from the fact that the check-in staff, gate employees, and flight attendants are almost always overtly kind and friendly, JetBlue pilots also get into the service side of the action. It is not uncommon to see a pilot help out with the cleanup inside the plane in order to speed up the turnaround time.

On one particular flight I was on, the pilot came out of the cockpit just before leaving the gate and addressed the passengers using the microphone. He said, "Thank you very much for flying with us today. I am sure you will enjoy the JetBlue **experience**. By show of hands, how many of you are first-time flyers with JetBlue?"

Truth
NUMBER

8

Gaining Buy-in
Is the Only
Way to Execute
a Brand
Strategy

None of us raised our hands even though there probably were a few first-time JetBlue flyers. The pilot continued, "Great! We have a bunch of savvy veterans who have come back for the JetBlue **experience**. Then you know what to expect. Great service, a great flight, and live TV. Folks, today we have the best flight attendants in the industry. Please don't hesitate to reach out to them if there is anything we can do to make your **experience** with us as pleasant as possible."

In less than 15 seconds, this pilot not only mentioned the term "experience" three times, he also set a high expectation for the flight attendants to live up to. My guess is that they welcomed that high expectation because they truly enjoy servicing passengers. JetBlue does a phenomenal job hiring, training, and evaluating its employee base to ensure they buy into the strategy and deliver it at each customer touchpoint.

Drafting optimal behaviors requires a unique investment by your company. In return, doing so promises to maximize the strategic value of workforce performance and contribute to a sustainable competitive advantage. As I said earlier, Southwest Airlines (in 2004) had 225,895 applications for 1,706 positions. Why? Because Southwest is a great employer that delivers great experiences. The best employee candidates want to be part of a company like Southwest and JetBlue. Make creating behaviors and managing them the highest priority effort in your company!

The following Ideas Into Action section will break down a process for building proprietary behaviors.

Bottom line: The behaviors that your employees create become proprietary and lead to differentiation in the marketplace. Behaviors are the way you do business. They drive your culture. They drive your brand from the inside out.

Truth
NUMBER

Gaining Buy-in
Is the Only
Way to Execute
a Brand
Strategy

IDEAS ⟶ ACTION

"The most effective and enjoyable way for most of us to cope with change is to help create it."

BUILD A BRAND-DRIVEN PERFORMANCE SYSTEM

Most companies go about managing performance in ways that are guaranteed to produce less than optimal results. They establish reward programs that affect only a select few and therefore quickly lose steam. They establish policies to discourage bad behaviors rather than celebrate desired behaviors, or they make the mistake of not holding managers accountable for conducting performance evaluations that are in alignment with the strategy.

How can leadership manage success rather than leave it up to chance? How can you as a leader be proactive in utilizing the company's talents and brand strategy to ensure success? You must incorporate your company's brand concepts into the human resource systems, turning HR from a cost-reducing function into one that has its eye on managing talent. Doing so will dramatically increase the probability that your employees' interests are aligned with those of the company (the brand).

ACHIEVING BRAND INTEGRITY PERFORMANCE SUCCESS PROGRAM

To successfully integrate your company's Brand Lens concepts into your HR performance systems, you must make the brand the focus of your company. Doing so will clarify for employees what is expected of them in their day-to-day actions and communications.

At Brand Integrity, we call this an *Achieving Brand Integrity Performance Success* program. It's a proven way to manage performance based on powerful behavioral principles for bringing out the best in people, whether as individuals, teams, business units, or as an organization.

Reasons to use your brand to drive performance are simple and difficult to dispute. An *Achieving Brand Integrity Performance Success* program will:

Truth
NUMBER

8

Gaining Buy-in
Is the Only
Way to Execute
a Brand
Strategy

• Provide an opportunity to link your company's unique brand concepts to each job description in the company, allowing you to clearly communicate expectations (clarifies expectations for performance).

• Allow each employee to internalize Brand Competencies and behaviors that they will be responsible for bringing to life, and provide a simple approach for measuring success (personalizes the brand concepts).

• Help each employee better understand the impact he or she has on business success for the company, instilling greater pride that enhances productivity (engages and enrolls employees in your strategy).

• Inspire and motivate each employee to deliver on-brand experiences that will drive the desired culture for your company and lead to lower turnover and increased productivity (establishes understanding and commitment to the brand concepts).

• Provide a framework for conducting performance evaluations that will ensure that each employee is contributing to the success of the company (infuses accountability).

• Ensure that each employee is living the brand consistently across all functional areas and geographic boundaries (leads to buy-in across the organization).

"Consistency
is king."

174

The *Achieving Brand Integrity Performance Success* program is a proven methodology for building Brand Competencies and brand-driven behaviors in six steps or fewer. The following table provides a high-level, step-by-step view of our approach. This approach is unique in that employees are engaged in the process of developing the performance expectation (within the confines of the documented strategy, of course). By utilizing peer development, the Brand Integrity approach enables employees to put the behavior expectation together in their own words (prior to legal check), which leads to much greater buy-in.

Truth
NUMBER

Gaining Buy-in
Is the Only
Way to Execute
a Brand
Strategy

! Achieving Performance Success	**Ensure long-term success by:** • Implementing periodic self-evaluations. • Integrating behaviors into performance reviews.
6 Leadership Review Session	Review the results with job category leaders to: • Ensure changes have retained original intentions. • Obtain leadership buy-in on final behaviors.
5 Personalization Session	Conduct a modified, efficient approach to: • Customize behaviors for similar positions. • Leverage existing behaviors for positions with only a few people.
4 Buy-in/Kickoff Workshop	Work with employees of the job category to: • Understand brand behaviors. • Gain commitment. • Ensure ability to take action.
3 Peer Development Interactive Session	Work with top performers in the job category to: • Build brand behaviors. • Uncover obstacles that make doing the behaviors a challenge.
2 Must-have Session	Meet with the leaders of the job category to: • Understand Brand Competencies. • Determine "must-have" brand behaviors.
1 Project Planning and Kickoff	Plan for success: • Collect brand strategy behaviors. • Integrate job description behaviors.

For a detailed breakdown of the steps required to build an *Achieving Brand Integrity Performance Success* program, go to www.brandintegrity.com/truth8.

CLOSE THE PERFORMANCE GAP

Truth
NUMBER

8

Gaining Buy-in
Is the Only
Way to Execute
a Brand
Strategy

The brand strategy is visible. You can see employees' behaviors. You know whether they are delivering the experiences customers desire. It's time to focus on closing the gap between your top performers and bottom performers.

Think of poor performance in your company as a debilitating disease. If you had a debilitating disease in your body, you wouldn't ignore it. You would take proactive measures to fix it. However, when poor performance arises in a business, some leaders act as if it's not happening, or maybe it will fix itself over time, or worse, they feel as if they can live with it as long as it doesn't get worse.

To sustain a brand strategy, you cannot take this approach. Doing so is contradictory to the beliefs and behaviors that make up the operational definition of the brand strategy. Doing so will validate a misalignment in management's commitment to DOING the brand strategy.

To build a brand-driven work culture, leaders must develop a great sense of urgency when dealing with poor performance on their team. They must recognize that the poorest of performers (the weakest links) will ultimately influence how successful the company will be and how quickly the company will reach the business goals and objectives.

Dealing with poor performance requires emotional strength. Emotionally weak leaders often lack the necessary confidence and discipline to hold employees accountable and lack the sensitivity to communicate effectively. Lack of emotional strength is the number-one reason leaders fail to deal appropriately with poor-performing employees.

Poor performance for a brand-driven organization can be defined as any performance that is off-brand or average to below average with no indication of positive changes.

176

Some leaders use the excuse that letting a poor performer go would leave them shorthanded or in a difficult predicament in which others would need to pick up the additional extra workload. For those excuse-laden leaders, I offer up this reality check: if your great performers are forced to work with poor performers, they are most likely already being overworked and are frustrated with having to pick up the slack.

In thinking through how to effectively deal with poor performers in your company, ask yourself these five important questions:

Truth
NUMBER
8
Gaining Buy-in
Is the Only
Way to Execute
a Brand
Strategy

1. Are there people on your team who are not performing up to the expectations for the job?

   • Over time, the poor performers ultimately hinder the productivity of even the best employees.

2. Are you walking the talk regarding your brand strategy?

   • Are your top performers listening to you preach about the brand and its values and benefits, only to witness poor performers getting by just as easily as before? Leaders who allow poor performers to ride the coattails of the strongest members of the team will ultimately lose credibility.

3. Are there members of your team whom you would not hire again if given the opportunity?

   • If so, you are losing the war on poor performance. There are three ways to handle this situation:

     - Inspire the individual to learn what it will take to become a great performer.

     - Motivate the individual to try another position within the company where his/her energy and skill may be better suited.

     - Terminate the individual who does not positively represent the company's brand and who does not have what it takes to live it in his/her daily work.

       Rarely do leaders fire someone and then say, "I wish I had kept him/her a little longer." In fact, most often they wonder why they didn't do it a lot sooner.

4. Do your people know how they're doing?

- Great leaders don't allow employees to wonder. If they are doing great, these leaders let them know. If they are doing just okay, they let them know. And if performance is hindering progress, they let them know that, too. Leaders must care enough to confront performance, otherwise they risk losing the respect of their top performers.

5. Do you set realistic expectations for success and attach deadlines for success?

- When someone isn't performing as expected, you have to take the time, energy, and focus to redefine for that person what success looks like and establish a benchmark for accountability. Doing so will instill the urgency and focus required for the employee to have the greatest opportunity for success.

Good employees will try hard to meet performance objectives if they know what good performance is!

Keep in mind that culture transformation does not happen overnight. It takes two to three years of consistent energy and focus on making sure employees understand and are committed to doing the required behaviors. Your company should expect to invest time and resources to ensure that your performance program is well executed.

The rewards are great! Build a brand-driven work culture by integrating the brand concepts into a performance program and watch the key result areas skyrocket. You'll gain:

- Happier and more productive employees.
- Greater customer loyalty, which leads to more repeat purchases.
- Increased sales to new customers.

In Truth #9, you'll gain further insight into another way to build and sustain buy-in. Brace yourself. The title of this Truth is: *Most Companies Suck at Capturing Successes and Recognizing People.*

Truth
NUMBER
8

Gaining Buy-in
Is the Only
Way to Execute
a Brand
Strategy

178

Truth
NUMBER

Gaining Buy-in
Is the Only
Way to Execute
a Brand
Strategy

Truth
NUMBER

Most Companies Suck at Capturing Successes and Recognizing People

TOPICS

9.1 Reality of Recognition in the Workplace

9.2 Why Reward Programs Don't Work

9.3 Peer-to-Peer Recognition Drives Strategy Alignment and Company Performance

9.4 Success Stories That Motivate Action

9.5 Bottom-line Impacts of Pervasive Recognition

IDEAS ⤏ ACTION

1 Implement an "I Caught You Living the Brand" Recognition Program	2 Conduct Celebrating Success Presentations and Workshops	3 Budget for Success

Truth
NUMBER

9

Most
Companies
Suck at
Capturing
Successes and
Recognizing
People

When meeting with executive leaders and business owners to discuss their business strategies and current challenges, one challenge almost always seems to come up over and over again. I ask leaders how their strategies are promoted internally and, like clockwork, they complain about what a lousy job their organization does in recognizing employees' successes and sharing them with others. I can sum up hundreds of similar conversations in one sentence: "We are great at having successes, but we really struggle to capture them, recognize the people doing them, and share them with other employees in order to motivate and educate them to do the same."

The bad news is … most companies *do* suck at capturing successes and recognizing their people.

The good news is … this chapter provides great insight into ways to stop sucking.

9.1 Reality of Recognition in the Workplace

The reality of recognition in the workplace is that **much** more is needed. Period.

STRATEGIC RECOGNITION

For a brand-driven, strategic company, the recognition strategy should be to acknowledge and reward employees based on performance-related criteria rather than other factors such as years of service. A more strategic approach to leveraging recognition is not only doable, it's simple. And it's a **must** if you expect to delight your employees and motivate them to deliver the experiences you know your customers want.

Recognition should be a strategic, leadership-driven process for acknowledging others in the workplace for good work that is aligned with the overall business objectives and strategies of the company. Yes, I mean *good* work, not just *great* work. I agree with Jim Collins, author of the book *Good to Great*, when he says that "often times *good* is the enemy of *great* [my italics]." However, one of my business partners, Frederick Beer (who happens to be as smart as Jim Collins) makes the following claim: "The number one cause of decreased productivity in corporate America is a lack of recognition for good work." That's right, *good* work. Let's face it, not everyone is capable of doing *great* work. In fact, many people aren't. Nevertheless, *good* work can be done by all when they put their minds to it. The sad reality is that most employees don't consistently focus on trying to be good.

> *"The number one cause of decreased productivity in corporate America is a lack of recognition for good work."* —Frederick Beer

There are two types of recognition (or lack thereof) that your company should be paying attention to:

1. Intellectual recognition.

2. Emotional recognition.

Intellectual recognition occurs when an employee is recognized for the knowledge they have and their willingness to share it. In today's knowledge-driven economy, this type of recognition becomes a differentiator for companies looking to outsmart and outperform the competition. When organizations like yours, or those you compete with, don't provide the intellectual recognition employees need, knowledge-sharing decreases and expertise becomes limited. Eventually, individuals begin to hoard their ideas, thwarting creative thinking and idea development. In companies like this, you can count on employees to shoot down one another's ideas, rejecting them before even really seeking to understand them. This happens because of a lack of intellectual recognition. It's a natural human defense mechanism: employees kill ideas and suggestions just as theirs were killed or ignored in the past.

On the other end of the spectrum is emotional recognition, in which employees should feel connected to the brand strategy and understand their impact on executing it. When you do a good job of recognizing

SOLUTION

"STOP! Gather the successes. Share them with all employees. Keep sharing them over time. It's a great way to educate employees on what behaviors and experiences you're looking for."

employees for behaviors that drive your brand strategy, you raise their emotional level, which helps them be more engaged and ready to do what it takes to reach your key company objectives. On the flip side, a lack of emotional recognition is a surefire way to disengage your people and cause them to feel less appreciated, which diminishes alignment and consensus on the importance of the brand strategy. Even worse, you'll be able to count on these disengaged employees to drag their feet on company initiatives. In some cases, without adequate emotional investment, employees will counteract your strategy by resisting the necessary behaviors and experiences that would bring it to life.

Truth
NUMBER

9

Most
Companies
Suck at
Capturing
Successes and
Recognizing
People

EMPLOYEES ARE DISENGAGING

Do you believe your employees are willing to go the extra mile for you and your company solely for their paycheck? Are they so highly committed to seeing that your company does well that they'll put in whatever extra effort is needed, day in and day out, to ensure their jobs get done and done right? If you believe this, you're either running an amazing company or you're slightly delusional. If you're the former, hats off to you. Keep doing what you're doing with respect to recognizing your employees.

"Okay, what's the next priority ...?"   *"What will I have for dinner tonight? I can't wait for American Idol!"*

According to a global study by Towers Perrin, a human resources company, only 14 percent of employees are "fully engaged" in their work. The study consisted of more than 85,000 people working for mid- to large-size companies in 16 countries across the globe. It concluded that the majority of employees are only moderately engaged or, worse yet, actively *disengaged*.

The survey also concluded that 43 percent of respondents admitted to being "passive job seekers," meaning they would be open to job offers from other companies.

Employees who are not satisfied with their jobs either quit and move on (which is bad) or quit and stay but don't tell anyone they're dissatisfied (which is much, much worse). How many of your employees have quit on the job? How sure are you about your answer? Studies show your guess is most likely quite low. They may come to work each day, but in reality they're not engaged, inspired, or motivated to accomplish great things. They've mentally quit, yet they continue to weigh down your company, take from your payroll, and reduce your bottom line. Sounds scary, doesn't it? Well, for most company leaders this is a day-to-day reality, whether they know it or not. Towers Perrin's study shows that, most likely, 86 percent of your people fall into this category to differing degrees.

I'm not trying to ruin your day here. I'm being a realist. Honestly, I'm not the guy who spits in the punch bowl at the company party, trying to ruin the fun for everyone else. I'm just making sure that before you gulp down another cup of punch, you know what you're drinking.

Here are some facts to back up my claim that employees are disengaging more than ever before:

• Fifty-seven percent of workers in the United States think that tenure determines pay where they work. Only 35 percent believe performance is the deciding factor.

• The United States is losing between $292 and $355 billion annually due to the lack of productivity from actively disengaged employees.

- Personal fulfillment at work drives productivity. Studies of productivity conclude that, for jobs of low, medium, and high complexity, highly motivated employees were respectively 52 percent, 85 percent, and 127 percent more productive than employees who had average motivation. Now, for a moment, consider the cost to your company of having disengaged employees.

Truth
NUMBER
9
Most
Companies
Suck at
Capturing
Successes and
Recognizing
People

Here's the kicker:

- Three out of ten workers planned to look for new job opportunities in 2006, and 41 percent plan on jumping ship by the end of 2007.

The Internet has made job-hunting while on the job so easy. As if worrying about employees shopping online, looking at obscene pictures, chatting via instant messaging, receiving and writing endless personal e-mails, and surfing for their own entertainment wasn't enough, now company leaders need to worry about these employees searching for better work opportunities and firing off dozens of resumes during their work shift.

If you're thinking we should turn off the Internet, you're missing the point. Browsing the Web is a symptom of the underlying problem. If you stop the symptom, you can be assured that another one will eventually appear. In a recent survey by Salary.com, employees admitted to wasting 2.09 hours per day, excluding lunch and breaks. Last time I checked, the average workday in America was about eight hours. So this suggests that the average employee is not present for more than 25 percent of their workday.

I promise that if your employees are disengaged for 25 percent of their time, there is no way you will consistently outperform a competitor that is able to engage and motivate its people.

BRAND CHALLENGE

"We've tried reward programs to motivate our people but they always seem to lose steam quickly."

Okay, here are three *true* opinions to support the above stated facts. These opinions are true and they make complete logical sense.

Please judge for yourself. If you disagree, please call me to discuss: 585-442-5404.

1. Employees typically want to do good work, but are held back for three reasons:

   - They don't understand the company brand strategy or how to *do* it.

   - They're not consistently recognized for a job well done, which makes it hard for them to know when they're doing things right. This also makes it difficult for them to have a feeling of accomplishment and pride in their work.

   - They're in the wrong job for their personality and skills.

2. Recognizing employees consistently for doing the right behaviors, delivering the right experiences, and helping to achieve company objectives will dramatically enhance:

   - Operational efficiencies and employee productivity.

   - Loyalty of your employees and customers.

   - New sales to existing customers and prospects.

3. The number one cause of decreased productivity is a lack of recognition for doing a *good* job.

The facts are clear. The reason employees stay loyal to a company is that they feel appreciated for a job well done. Inversely, the reason employees leave is because they don't feel appreciated. This is supported by a U.S. Department of Labor statistic citing lack of appreciation as the number-one reason people leave their jobs.

9.2 Why Reward Programs Don't Work

I'm sorry to be so negative early on in this chapter. However, facts are facts. Employee appreciation is not only the most sought-after benefit for the average employee (almost always ranked higher than compensation), it's also one of the most challenging activities for companies to implement consistently.

Truth
NUMBER

9

Most Companies Suck at Capturing Successes and Recognizing People

SOLUTION

"Implement a recognition program focused on behaviors and experiences — not just bottom-line results. That way, more employees can be recognized for doing the important things that make your company successful."

Most companies resort to reward and recognition programs that simply don't work. Please notice that I reference these programs as reward (first), then recognition. These programs have a fundamentally flawed view of human behavior that focuses on the carrot and the stick. What happens when the carrot is removed? Or the boss's back is turned? Or your competitor offers a greater reward opportunity?

Truth
NUMBER

9

Most
Companies
Suck at
Capturing
Successes and
Recognizing
People

The truth is every person in the company should be recognized, even if only a few are actually rewarded. To truly achieve both short- and long-term performance successes, companies should implement recognition (first) and reward (second) programs that make it easy for all employees to participate.

So why do reward programs fail? Most fail for at least one of three reasons. The reasons and the associated results are in the following table.

Why Your Reward Program Failed	Result of Your Failing Reward Program
Too exclusive, leading to limited participation.	• Same people win time and again. • Short life cycles of programs lead to cynicism towards flavor-of-the-month-type activity. • Manager favoritism. • Unhealthy work culture filled with underachievement and backstabbing. Often a dichotomy can form between the haves and the have-nots with respect to recognition and reward.
Difficult to manage (beyond sales incentive programs).	• Expensive: lots of people-time and financial commitment. • Rewarding results, not behaviors. • Cumbersome to track.
Focused too much on financial targets at the exclusion of the right behaviors required to hit targets.	• De-motivates more employees than it motivates. • Decreases teamwork focused on company success. Increases individual motivation focused on individual success. • Leads to missed opportunities to recognize good behaviors that drive financial results. • Motivates some short-term success and causes long-term division between groups of employees.

Exclusivity that squashes participation and kills the work culture:

A telecom company with the typical Presidents Club-type reward program for salespeople who hit their targets has created a dichotomy of work cultures: the sales side and the administration/sales support side. Because there's no process to recognize the support people, there's as much resentment about the success of the company as there is excitement. Salespeople are rewarded and recognized for their efforts while support people are disenfranchised. What do you think this does to employee morale, productivity, and willingness to go the extra mile to help close the next big deal?

The costly reward program that needs full-time people to manage it:

A hospital that employs more than 5,000 people has a Catch Them Doing It Right-type program where employees, patients, and patients' loved ones can nominate people for anything they deem appropriate. This ill-defined, non-strategic program requires employees to read and subjectively evaluate tons of nominations on a monthly basis. Tracking these nominations, subjectively choosing the best ones (because they're not linked to strategic objectives of the hospital), and bringing together the chosen winners for a monthly luncheon will cost this hospital a small fortune over the next few years. And, even still, 80 percent or more of the employee base will never recognize anyone or be recognized.

I hit my target and am off to Hawaii:

A manufacturing company that offers a trip incentive has a sales guy who misrepresents his company's product and delivery time so that he can close the big deal that enables him to hit the financial target necessary to win the trip to Hawaii. This guy is on the beach while his company figures out how to deliver upon his promises. And the customer becomes dissatisfied because they are not really getting what they thought they were buying. This costs the company money and diminishes employee and customer loyalty — and the salesperson got rewarded for this behavior, encouraging him or her to do it again.

Truth
NUMBER

Most Companies Suck at Capturing Successes and Recognizing People

Reward programs *can* work if they are driven by the spirit of recognition and are less focused on the reward. Therefore, let's call it a *recognition program* from here on out.

Here are some solutions to rejuvenate your recognition efforts, or to help guide a new initiative. First, make the recognition program about the company strategy and key objectives and provide detailed behaviors that employees should be doing. Don't make it just about company or individual financial goals. Make sure employees *understand* the strategy, objectives, and behaviors; are *committed* to achieving them (true belief, not just lip service); and know how to take *action* to achieve results.

Second, make sure both employees and leaders focus on finding successes and sharing them with others. Individual successes that lead to company results are critical input for any recognition program.

Last, make the reward a trophy award, not cash. I'm not suggesting that you immediately shut down your current reward programs and provide mall gift cards. You can't do that because in all likelihood your reward earners are depending on their winnings and bonuses as a part of their compensation. However, keep in mind, they may see these rewards as entitlement, not as motivation. Are you still wondering why most reward programs fail?

What I'm suggesting is that over time you wean employees away from cash rewards and more toward awards with longer-lasting impacts. (My disclaimer here is that if you are a sales organization that depends on sales contests, don't change a thing. And by the way, I don't claim to be an expert in sales contests. However, your company should consider a recognition program that involves more than just the sales team.)

Let's get one thing straight before going any further: money is not the number one motivator for the majority of employees.

I realize that, in some cases, there are jobs where the "hunting dogs" go out and hunt 100 percent motivated by the money they can earn in commissions. However, for most people in the workforce, a simple pat on the back for a job well done has repeatedly been proven a greater source of motivation for better performance. Studies supporting this fact have been done for years. Even so, many leaders still find it hard to believe. For those of you who may doubt my claim that less than 10 percent of employees are primarily motivated by money, let's say that I'm off by a factor of three. Let's say, for you naysayers, that 30 to 35 percent of employees are truly motivated by money first. That

"Consistency is king."

still leaves 65 to 70 percent of your employees who find greater satisfaction from consistent and sincere appreciation for a job well done than they do from cold, hard cash.

Now, I admit that you will rarely find employees who would turn down a cash award. Why would they? But from a business perspective, your question should be whether cash is the best motivator. Again, study after study says it's not.

Trophy-value merchandise is a better motivator than cash. A trophy is a tangible representation of an achievement that elicits pride in its owner. The concept of trophy value is quite simple. If an employee earns a $500 TV, it will sit proudly in the living room for five to 10 years and serve as a constant reminder of a job well done. Give this same employee $500 in cash and it's unlikely he will use the money to purchase an award for himself. Instead, he will probably just lump it in with his regular income and use it to make ends meet at the grocery store, the gas pump, or on a nagging credit card balance. In this case, the employee soon forgets the reward even happened. Or worse, he/she gets pissed off if the reward doesn't happen again, regardless of performance.

While both cash and non-cash awards have a place in the employee compensation mix, it's important to stress that cash can be an ineffective motivator. In most cases, it simply will not energize people to reach beyond their basic job requirements to achieve

SOLUTION

"Focus on trophy value, not cash value. Cash is spent at the grocery store by the end of the week. The Bahamas trip is gone after it is used. The flat-screen TV from your recognition program stays in their living room for a decade or more, continuously reminding them of their efforts to grow your company."

good results. Trophy-value awards fill the need that cash cannot buy — the symbol of achievement and success, social acceptance at work, approval for a job well done, and increased self-esteem from recognition throughout the company.

Trophy-value awards fill the need
that cash cannot buy.

Truth
NUMBER

9

Most
Companies
Suck at
Capturing
Successes and
Recognizing
People

Bottom line: If your recognition program is to truly motivate your people across, up, and down your organization, then cash is NOT the most effective reward.

9.3 Peer-to-Peer Recognition Drives Strategy Alignment and Company Performance

So, reward clearly does not need to mean more money. One of the biggest contributing factors to a more satisfying work life is the quality of relationships with others. Right there at the top of the motivation ladder is being noticed for doing good work. But feedback doesn't pay the bills, so a thoughtful balance must be struck between recognition of good work and compensation that reflects it.

Your people need to see that they can get where they want to be by doing behaviors that lead to great customer experiences. The good news is that behaviors are not set in stone. The bad news is that habits tend to be very hard to break. It takes time to change habits, but it happens if you accentuate the positives through recognition and rewards that can be applied consistently and genuinely. Using the brand strategy as the fulcrum, you can help break old habits and replace them with habits that build the brand.

"Consistency
is king."

The good news is that behaviors can be changed overnight.
The bad news is that habits can't.

192

Initially, no one really owns the brand. That's why so few typically live it in their daily behaviors. People don't get territorial or defensive when you suggest that everyone rally around the brand. When you educate employees and empower them to live the brand, you create alignment and freedom for them to exercise great judgment. You set them up to succeed and when you do, your customers' loyalty will increase and your brand image will be enhanced. With focus, teamwork, and regular recognition and reward, attitudes — and thus behaviors — will change and your brand will begin to drive a more positive, performance-oriented culture. Then, everyone will be happy!

Truth
NUMBER

9

Most
Companies
Suck at
Capturing
Successes and
Recognizing
People

The best way to get to this euphoric state, a state of complete strategic alignment throughout your company, is through a peer-to-peer recognition program. Peer-to-peer recognition is not a new idea. It's an old idea that, when done right, is the best investment you can make in your people. It's an inexpensive way to motivate and retain workers by empowering them to thank and show appreciation to coworkers for a job well done. Often, this can be done with a simple card or e-mail.

A peer-to-peer recognition program is the best investment you can make in your people.

Mercer Human Resource Consulting estimates about 35 percent of major companies have some sort of peer recognition program, a 10 percent increase from five years ago. The recessionary time of the early new millennium years led to fewer pay raises and many more companies found peer-to-peer recognition programs to be a more affordable way to motivate and retain employees.

A nice thing about a well-designed peer-to-peer program is that it provides an opportunity for all employees to participate. A frontline worker can have a say in who is rewarded regardless of hierarchy in the company. So by peer-to-peer, I am referring to any employee recognizing the good work of others (behaviors in alignment with the brand strategy) up, down, and across the company. Again, peer-to-peer does not simply refer to employees of similar roles or hierarchy.

When done right, peer-to-peer recognition will focus on behavioral outcomes and not just end results. Employee behaviors that are powered by the brand strategy of the company should be what you encourage others to achieve. Behaviors are visible. Your coworkers can see if you are doing the right things. When they do, they should have a way to recognize you. If you don't tie your recognition program to behaviors, witnessing activities worthy of recognition can become very subjective and ineffective.

Truth

NUMBER

9

Most
Companies
Suck at
Capturing
Successes and
Recognizing
People

Remember, people are not your company's greatest asset. (See Truth #7: *Employees Are NOT Your Greatest Asset.*) The *right* people doing the *right* things are your greatest asset. A peer-to-peer recognition program is the best way to track and measure who is doing the right things most often. To create such a program, you'll need a systematic approach that is well-thought-out, clearly communicates expectations, eliminates bureaucracy, establishes objective recognition criteria, and offers relevant rewards to those who are recognized. In the Ideas Into Action section of this chapter, you will find an overview of Brand Integrity's *Achieving Brand Integrity Recognition* program, along with the steps for developing a sustainable recognition approach.

Understand this final thought about peer-to-peer recognition programs: these programs are often the best way to close the "knowing-doing gap" that exists in most companies. The gap between an employee *knowing* what behaviors to do and actually *doing* them can be shrunk by executing a recognition program that recognizes and rewards doing the desired behaviors. Those who look for and recognize the right behaviors being done by others typically understand the why behind the strategy. They get the company's philosophies, brand values, and core beliefs. In most cases, these individuals have more of a passion for action: they are focused on doing. And for those who are caught demonstrating the right behaviors, well, they're doing them, aren't they? A sound peer-to-peer recognition program encourages employees to do the behaviors that bring the brand to life.

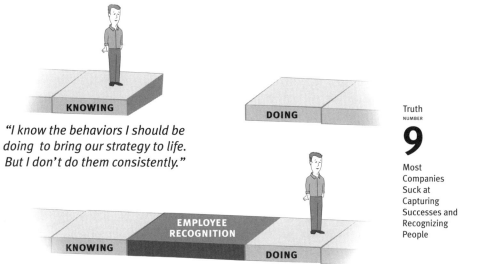

9.4 Success Stories That Motivate Action

Okay, so I'm going to assume that you read the beginning of this chapter and bought into the reality of recognition in the workplace. You then began to rethink your current and/or past failed attempts at reward programs that de-motivate the majority of your employees. Next, you began to think through how to implement a peer-to-peer recognition program that is open to all employees. Now, it's time to think about how to engage employees and inspire participation. I believe the best way to do this is through effective storytelling. I am not referring to storytelling as a deceptive way to portray the truth about what's happening in your company. I'm referring to storytelling as a way to engage your employees intellectually and emotionally by describing "living the brand" moments.

When it comes to highlighting and reporting the successes of your peer-to-peer recognition program, creating slide shows and charts to report who recognized whom for what won't be enough. Seek to involve people at a level that will truly inspire them. Avoid the hyperbolic company-speak that is generally developed by your corporate communications people. Motivational speeches about setting and meeting goals might engage your team on an intellectual level, but it will not inspire their hearts and minds. If you want to persuade them, present success stories about individuals living the brand, doing the right behaviors, and achieving bottom-line impacts. Unite them with ideas that strike an emotional chord. You can weave a ton of information into a story based on what we call the evidence. The evidence is when one peer recognizes another for a "living the brand" moment. With the right background and clearly communicated success, you can pack a story with emotional power to ensure it becomes a memorable and educational moment. Doing so engages employees on a whole new level.

Truth
NUMBER

9

Most
Companies
Suck at
Capturing
Successes and
Recognizing
People

The process for using evidence to document a success story is as easy as drafting a short case study:

Step 1: Outline the challenge and/or situation that led up to the living-the-brand moment(s). List the participants in the story and their roles. Provide as much detail as possible to make the challenge or situation a compelling one.

Step 2: Document the evidence (behaviors) delivered by the participant(s). Be as specific as possible in describing behaviors performed and benefits delivered.

Step 3: Document the living-the-brand evidence that made the moment (story) a success. Document what the behaviors and benefits led to from an experiential perspective. Make sure to include the bottom-line impact that resulted from the evidence. If the outcome helped to strengthen a Brand Lens concept, core value, or business principle of your company, be sure to feature it in this last section of the story. Include impacts such as increased efficiencies or productivity, new cross-selling opportunities, additional sales to new customers, or enhanced loyalty of existing customers.

These stories can be shared at company events, in newsletters, posted to the intranet, or simply shared by leaders at the water cooler. The more formalized you make the process of gathering successes and sharing them, the greater involvement you can expect from employees.

Catching others doing the right behaviors and experiences and sharing those successes is the best way to educate employees on the company strategy, generate their commitment, and stimulate positive actions.

Truth
NUMBER

9

Most
Companies
Suck at
Capturing
Successes and
Recognizing
People

For an outline of the Brand Integrity Success Story process, visit www.brandintegrity.com/truth9.

9.5 Bottom-line Impacts of Pervasive Recognition

All this recognition talk sure does sound good but what's the real impact of doing it? As stated previously, it will drive a more productive workforce. However, this concept alone is typically not enough to get executive leaders to really take a hard look at the potential of a peer-to-peer recognition program to enhance company success. At a minimum, you should expect the following results from a well-designed and managed peer-to-peer recognition program that includes a strong success story component:

• **Greater employee engagement:** Your employees will become more engaged, inspired, and motivated to behave in ways that drive loyalty (employee and customer) and sales. They'll become more engaged just from having an opportunity to enhance their understanding of and involvement with the company strategy.

• **Increased employee productivity:** Your employees will become more productive. This will happen as a result of their knowing the strategy and knowing how they impact productivity, loyalty, and sales for the company.

- **Stronger leadership:** Your leadership will have a strategic tool that will enable them to identify, measure, and recognize behaviors and experiences that increase company sales and bottom-line results.

- **Greater employee focus:** Your employees will become more focused on executing the company strategy, ensuring better accuracy and consistency in delivering it.

Truth
NUMBER

9

Most
Companies
Suck at
Capturing
Successes and
Recognizing
People

- **Enhanced company-wide performance mind-set:** Your entire company will become more passionate about achieving successful performance as opposed to focusing on receiving rewards. Work will become more meaningful as employees are recognized for doing good work that makes a difference in the success of the company — a difference they can truly relate to and appreciate.

Your peer-to-peer recognition program (like any brand-driven strategic initiative) should be held accountable to drive bottom-line performance in the following three areas:

1. Increased productivity of employees.

2. Enhanced loyalty of employees and customers.

3. Increased sales to existing and new customers.

Ultimately, these all lead to increased revenue and increased profits.

The result of pervasive recognition is a performance culture driven by employees who have a performance mind-set.

- **Performance culture:** Your employees can recognize success in themselves and others. They consistently produce the behaviors that you as a leader are looking for.

- **Performance mind-set:** Your employees understand the required behaviors, the experiences they should deliver, *and* the impact they have on the success of the company.

BRAND CHALLENGE

"We've tried implementing reward programs and have struggled to get the majority of the employees to participate."

Fortunately for you, your competition probably sucks at capturing successes and recognizing their people. They don't have a program or the insight from the Ideas Into Action section you are about to read.

IMPLEMENT AN "I CAUGHT YOU LIVING THE BRAND" RECOGNITION PROGRAM

Are you familiar with the Chinese proverb, "I hear and I forget. I see and I remember. I do and I understand"? This proverb embodies an important fact that some companies have proven true through the strategic implementation of a peer-to-peer, brand-driven recognition program: a recognition approach in the spirit of "I caught you doing something right." In this case, the "doing something right" part consists of demonstrating brand-driven behaviors and delivering branded experiences for colleagues, partners, and/or customers; behaviors and experiences that align with your overall strategy and company objectives.

Truth
NUMBER

9

Most Companies Suck at Capturing Successes and Recognizing People

Developing an "I Caught You Living the Brand" recognition program will help you to educate, inspire, and empower employees

"Consistency is king."

while holding them accountable for results. The purpose of this program will be to engage your workforce in **consistently** executing your company's brand strategy. What makes this approach unique is quite simple and difficult to refute. As the name suggests, "I Caught You" means that your employees need to recognize their peers. Therefore, those who recognize others should be recognized themselves. In fact, you should

recognize the Witnesses even more that the actual Brand Steward who was caught delivering the brand behavior and/or subsequent branded experience.

Think about this scenario for a moment: I catch you delivering amazing customer service as defined in our company's brand strategy. I nominate you by filling out an "I Caught You Living the Brand" nomination form and sending it to your manager for approval. Once approved, I receive six points for catching you and you receive four points for doing the right behavior/delivering the on-brand experience.

Then we can each redeem our points in exchange for merchandise online. Critical to the success of this type of program is to provide an incentive to the Witness.

Keep in mind we're trying to achieve buy-in with this program. Buy-in is achieved when employees understand the strategy, commit to it, and *do* it (See Truth #8: *Gaining Buy-in Is the Only Way to Execute a Brand Strategy*). If an employee can see the brand-driven behaviors and experiences being done by others, they themselves have reached the understanding stage. By nominating someone, they are demonstrating commitment to the strategy. At the same time, the Brand Steward is doing the behavior and being recognized for taking the right actions.

Truth
NUMBER
9
Most
Companies
Suck at
Capturing
Successes and
Recognizing
People

As participation in this type of program begins to increase, more employees than ever before will be buying into your brand strategy. You will have achieved the purpose stated above that is worth repeating: the engagement of your employees in consistent execution of your company's brand strategy.

"Consistency is king."

Conduct Celebrating Success Presentations and Workshops

As part of your recognition efforts, all employees up, down, and across your company must have an opportunity to interact with the program. The best way to do this is to put together a presentation and an interactive workshop experience where employees can come together to learn not only what other employees are accomplishing as noted through the evidence gathered, but also how they are accomplishing it. Therefore, more detail is needed to provide the necessary story behind the success. I recommend that you organize a minimum of two facilitated events per year with the objectives of celebrating successes, stimulating continued employee participation in the program, and further recognizing and rewarding employees who are delivering results (Witnesses and Brand Stewards). While it's okay to hire an outside facilitator to help out with these presentations and workshops, they should ultimately be led by you.

At these workshops, you will want to stick to the theme of gaining buy-in by looking for ways to share successes that will enhance understanding, lead to a greater commitment to participate, and stimulate immediate action in the days ahead.

> For a breakdown of Brand Integrity's approach for designing and delivering Celebrating Success Workshops, go to www.brandintegrity.com/truth9. There you will find ideas on how to structure your celebrating success activities to maximize buy-in.

BUDGET FOR SUCCESS

Hopefully you've made up your mind to begin an "I Caught You Living the Brand" recognition program and follow it up with a series of Celebrating Success Workshops. Now you need to figure out how to pay for all of this stuff. If you are like most leaders, you don't have a budget item that covers these activities. At least, you think you don't.

I will now prove to you with very logical insight that you have more than you need to pay for your recognition activities. The money should come from some familiar budgets: marketing, sales, recruitment, human resources, and training. Oh, and one more — the most nebulous of all — the CEO budget. The one budget that most leaders in an organization know little about, but they know it is there.

I'm not asking you to steal from Peter to pay Paul here. I'm suggesting that you take a hard look at each of the budgets listed below and challenge yourself to agree with the logic I'm presenting.

1. Take it from marketing

A recognition program focused on the brand will decrease the amount of *saying* the marketing department needs to do. Quite simply, employees will be focusing more on doing the brand strategy, which will lead to better experiences for the customer. These satisfied customers will become an unpaid marketing department for your company. In addition, a recognition program will become the most powerful internal communication tactic your company has ever had. An unpaid marketing department of raving fan customers and the most effective internal communications program and materials you can imagine are worthy of at least 25 percent of your marketing budget. For those marketers reading this, freaking out about all the creative and supposedly effective things you won't be able to do if you repurpose 25 percent of your budget, I ask that you just give it a try for one year. I promise you, after one year, you'll be glad to send a larger portion of your budget for this awesome internal brand development program.

Truth
NUMBER

9

Most
Companies
Suck at
Capturing
Successes and
Recognizing
People

2. Take it from sales

Your recognition program can be designed in ways to motivate all of your company's employees to become brand ambassadors, generating leads for the sales team. This will lead to more customers to pursue. Simply align your selling goals with the appropriate Brand Lens concept and begin holding your employee base accountable, at the very least, to try and generate leads. In addition, you could design in a cross-selling or repeat customer purchase component to your brand experience where employees can be educated on ways to stimulate more sales opportunities with current customers. These two activities alone are worthy of at least 10 percent of your sales budget.

3. Take it from human resources

Companies that implement peer-to-peer recognition programs that involve all employees are truly engaging in morale management. The "I Caught You" recognition program will lead to more energized and happier employees. This will decrease turnover (in most cases, dramatically), which will lead to decreased costs associated with losing employees and having to hire new ones. Make an estimate of how much lower you can take your turnover costs and apply that percentage to the recognition budget. Make it at least 10 percent. Don't forget how much a mis-hire can cost your company (up to 15 times base salary)!

4. Take it from recruitment

While this budget may be the same as human resources for many companies, it is still worth singling out because of the impact an "I Caught You" program can have on helping your company to find more of the right employees to help your company grow. Who needs a staffing agency when you have happy people who can help you find great prospects that are aligned with the brand values of your company? In much the same way as integrating sales development initiatives into your program, you can greatly reduce the cost of finding ideal employees by making this activity part of the behavior expectations. Just tie it to a Brand Lens concept and set the expectation regarding the recruitment behaviors you want to see from employees. Take 10 percent from your recruitment budget and plan to take more as your recruitment activity becomes less costly.

5. Take it from training

Do I really need to give you the logic on this one? The entire foundation of the "I Caught You" approach to recognition is based on the goal of educating employees on your company strategy. This program alone can dramatically enhance whatever efforts you have in place for orientation. You will be able to actually show the brand in action through success stories, workshops, and daily nominations with the program. Obviously you won't want to pull dollars from product and service training. However, any training you do on the company philosophy and orientation to the company values can be reallocated to the recognition program. Your investment here can go a lot further by showing and not just telling. Give the recognition budget the majority of your training dollars that would normally be spent on introducing a new employee or reminding existing employees about your company and its work culture.

Truth
NUMBER

Most
Companies
Suck at
Capturing
Successes and
Recognizing
People

6. Take it from the CEO

The recognition program will greatly enhance the leadership tools available to the CEO and his/her management team. By fostering teamwork, ensuring alignment of the overall brand strategy, and empowering leaders with opportunities to provide the much needed pat on the back for employees, CEOs will find the dollars from their "secret" budget to be wisely spent on recognizing the efforts of their people. For the CEO who needs better leadership skills with respect to empowering people and sharing successes, the recognition program will surely help him/her find his/her way. If the right employees doing the right things are really a company's greatest asset, then the majority of the CEO's budget should be repurposed to the recognition budget.

Truth

NUMBER

9

Most
Companies
Suck at
Capturing
Successes and
Recognizing
People

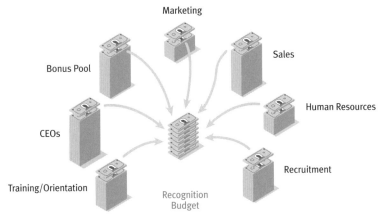

I've saved the best for last.

7. Take it from the bonus pool

For most companies, the number one source of dollars to be infused into the recognition budget should come from the annual bonus pool. The reason is quite simple: in most cases the annual bonus is a source of tension inside a company because leaders believe that bonuses paid out are egregiously inequitable. This happens because paying out bonuses is so subjective. Star performers don't really get the share they deserve, while mediocre and poor performers receive too much. Sound familiar? If you pay out a bonus to your employees based on company performance, then I bet it sounds all too familiar to you. To make matters worse, at the same time that you and your fellow leaders are grinding your teeth in frustration, your mediocre and poor performers believe that their bonus money is simply a payout for all of their hard work. These employees have a sense of entitlement that they deserve the bonus due to their efforts in driving the company's success (though they really don't).

"I can't believe I'm paying out this bonus to this underachiever. I HOPE he does better next year."

"Finally, this goes to cover my overtime."

To overcome the bonus payout quandary, simply take 10 to 20 percent of the company bonus pool for this year and apply it to the recognition budget. That way, your employees who are witnessing and *doing* the brand behaviors and experiences that are driving productivity, loyalty, sales, and ultimately profits will be the ones who receive a greater portion of the bonus. You'll find that over time you can shift much more of your bonus money to the recognition budget.

How much should you budget per employee to recognize good performance? There's no one right answer to this. With that said, you should invest at least one percent of what you pay to employ someone to recognize him or her for doing good work. Think about the total cost of an employee, including salary, taxes, and benefits. One percent of what you pay someone sure does seem like a safe, rational, and logical amount to use towards recognizing him or her for doing your company's brand strategy and driving positive financial results.

Truth
NUMBER

Only Leadership Has the Power to Ensure Brand Success

Truth
NUMBER

10

Only
Leadership
Has the Power
to Ensure
Brand Success

....

TOPICS

207

10.1 Commit to Aligning your People and Processes

Truth
NUMBER
10
Only
Leadership
Has the Power
to Ensure
Brand Success

Strong brands cannot be bought. They take time and incredible discipline to take root and grow in the minds of employees and customers. From reading this book, I hope you have taken to heart that the most overlooked (yet obvious) impact on brand-building success is people. The people who must be committed to delivering the practices and policies within your company have sole power over the strength of the brand. Since this is the case, be sure not to allow your company to over-commit budgets to marketing and sales without considering the necessary investment in talent management and process improvement. Make certain that your entire leadership team recognizes the need to align your people and processes with your brand strategy in order to avoid branding for the neighborhood!

Be sure not to invest too much time and energy in telling employees what and how to do their daily tasks without enough focus on explaining why. If you miss the ingredient of "why" then you ultimately miss the opportunity to make the brand meaningful to your employees.

Clearly build the connection for employees on why they need to follow specified processes and behave in certain ways. Spoon-feed them the *why*, and watch the alignment take hold.

Below are four things to consider for establishing powerful alignment throughout your workforce in ways that drive operational excellence (process):

1. Uncover and communicate beliefs.

Clearly define the beliefs and benefits of delivering on your brand promises in ways employees can understand. Involve them in the process and gain their perspective whenever possible. Remember this: their beliefs will drive their actions, which directly impact the delivery of your brand to other employees and customers.

BRAND CHALLENGE

"I can' t seem to get employees to do what I want them to do."

2. Educate and inspire.

Effectively communicate the impacts of employee actions (behaviors) in delivering your product or service so they understand the benefits received by customers. Build the business case. Make it as logical as possible. This will help employees understand the *why* behind their work.

3. Have patience.

This is the most overlooked, yet necessary ingredient for brand success. It takes time to educate and inspire employees and customers. Maintain a long-term view while taking pride in short-term results.

4. Maintain extreme focus.

Don't try to be all things to all people. More employees focused on delivering less processes and fulfilling fewer promises will lead to a much stronger brand. Remember, the essence of great brand strategy is sacrifice. Less is almost always more when it comes to making promises to be delivered for customers.

10.2 The Importance of Leadership Power

A few years ago I walked into Brand Integrity headquarters filled with excitement about a company I had just met, PAETEC Communications. The local start-up had already become a tremendous success story in the telecommunications industry. It had just been recognized as the second fastest growing company on the Deloitte Technology Fast 500 List. PAETEC had grown by 129,000 percent from 1998 to 2002, a time when most telecommunications companies had gone — or were in the process of going — bankrupt. The recessionary times of the early new millennium had hit this industry harder than most. I had just come from hearing PAETEC's CEO, Arunas Chesonis, speak at a conference and to say that I was very impressed would be a huge understatement. The work culture and sales success that Arunas described was nothing short of remarkable.

So I walked into the office and announced to my colleagues, "We have to get this company as a client!"

SOLUTION

"Focus on the why. Make sure employees understand WHY it is important to your customers and your company."

My sense was that a company, such as PAETEC, that was growing by the hundreds (150 to 1,100 employees in six years) was under the helm of a great leader and was bound to be encountering brand-building challenges that would eventually diminish the work culture if not properly managed.

Before you could spell PAETEC backwards, we had filled our whiteboard with lines, potential contacts, and connections that could serve as "Pathways to Power" (a.k.a., pathways to Arunas Chesonis). We obsessed over this strategy because we knew that the only way to get into a company like PAETEC and have a shot at selling an "executable" brand strategy was to have Arunas see it and love it. Without his support, we wouldn't be able to (or even want to) sell the strategy because it would not be able to be implemented from the top of the organization. Arunas represented the ultimate source of power at PAETEC, and only this type of power can ensure brand success. Fortunately for me, Arunas was motivated to ensure brand success for PAETEC. He has since published a book about the PAETEC story and the four PAETEC Brand Values make up each section.

My point in the above story is this: getting to the source of power in the organization is the ultimate challenge and also the ultimate *requirement* if you are truly going to have the opportunity to infect cultural change through an organizational brand strategy. If you are that source of power, don't try to delegate your brand strategy — your ultimate business strategy — to someone who doesn't have the ability to engage and motivate the rest of the company in truly meaningful, bottom-line enhancing work.

Only the leader has the power to ensure brand success, and there are two types of such power.

10.3 Two Types of Leadership Power

Leadership has two types of power that are absolutely required for brand strategy success. Whether you are a brand-building employee, consultant, or the very leader I am mentioning, pay careful attention to the logic behind both of these "power" perspectives:

1. The power to purchase.

Both knowledge and money are required to execute a brand strategy. Because a brand strategy is accountable for delivering top- and bottom-line business results, its buyers must be fully aware of the business plan, its objectives, and strategies. Sadly, all too often you'll find companies where even mid-level management isn't keenly aware of the business objectives, strategies, and tactics that are of highest priority. Instead, they are focused on their silo of accountability, lacking a view of the full picture of what success looks like. The leader of the company should and must know and communicate this information in order to justify investing in a culture-transforming brand strategy. Therefore, purchase power resides in the budget-influencing corner office.

2. The power to influence.

Executing a brand strategy requires focus, passion, and persistence. In today's ultra-competitive economy, company leaders struggle more than ever to keep their main lieutenants focused and on-strategy. The person responsible for executing a culture-transforming brand strategy must have the power and persistence to keep leaders and employees focused on strategy, day in and day out regardless of industry, product, or service changes. The core values of the company that help to make up the brand strategy must be constantly exuded by the leader.

The power to influence meets four distinct needs for organizations that want to execute a sustainable brand strategy:

1. The need for consciousness.

The leader of an organization has the ear and attention of other leaders and employees to help them become aware of the need for a brand strategy to improve the existing business realities. Leaders are well positioned to help others overcome their comfort with the status quo and to understand industry trends that may be out of their focused area of expertise or responsibility.

Truth
NUMBER

10

Only Leadership Has the Power to Ensure Brand Success

SOLUTION

"Tie the initiatives to the brand of the company so that they take on new meaning for employees."

2. The need for resources.

The leader has the power to reprioritize energy, commitment, and focus. Leaders can take the necessary control to reallocate both people and budgets, ensuring smart investment in the growth of the company.

3. The need for motivation.

Truth
NUMBER

10

Only
Leadership
Has the Power
to Ensure
Brand Success

The leader has the power to engage and inspire employees to embrace the brand strategy and deliver it through their attitudes and behaviors. Leaders can assign, direct, and manage the "change agents" who can create the necessary buzz about successes as they occur.

4. The need to overcome egos.

The leader has the power to overcome the number one challenge in executing a brand strategy: conquering internal politics caused by individuals whose beliefs are not aligned with those of the organization, or those who feel threatened by the brand strategy because of the feared impact it will have on their role and accountability. Only an organization's leader can ensure a "spirit of execution" in which people's hearts and minds are aligned to the point of cooperative, voluntary implementation of the strategy. When a strong leader is able to overcome the egos on executive row, those executives are able to proactively identify and influence the roles of the potential brand strategy supporters and detractors throughout the company.

10.4 A Final Message to CEOs: You Have the Power!

Let's face it: Your company cannot successfully implement a brand strategy without you as the brand champion. You have the ultimate power because you understand the whole package regarding the future growth of the company. You have your eyes and dollars on the desired brand image and the work culture that will help your company reach its financial goals. You as the leader need to ensure that the amazing brand strategy that is developed for your company is implemented and does not become a dust-collecting binder on your bookshelf. Implementing a successful brand strategy is your responsibility. Furthermore, it's your job. Get it done!

Truth
NUMBER

10

Only
Leadership
Has the Power
to Ensure
Brand Success

Notes

Truth 1: A Brand Strategy Is the Ultimate Business Strategy and Often the Least Understood

Page

20   "In the article entitled . . ." Lucas Conley, "Obsessive Branding Disorder," *Fast Company*, no. 99 (October 2005): 35.

22   "According to Spirit magazine . . ." Andrew C. Inkpen and Valerie DeGroot, "Southwest Airlines 2005," Thunderbird, The Garvin School of International Management, 2005.

28   "I believe in the philosophy . . ." Jim Collins, *Good to Great* (New York: Harper Collins, 2001).

29   "Professor Jim Doyle, who taught by MBA entrepreneurship class . . ." John Kotter, *Leading Change* (Boston, MA: Harvard Business School Press, 1996).

Truth 2: True Branding Is About Being Different, Not Saying Different Things

Page

40   "Cirque du Soleil changed the playing field . . ." Background on Cirque Du Soleil was found in the following:

- W. Chan Kim and Renée Mauborgne, *Blue Ocean Strategy: How to Create Uncontested Market Space and Make the Competition Irrelevant* (Harvard Business School Publishing Corporation, 2005)

- W. Chan Kim and Renée Mauborgne, "Blue Ocean Strategy," *Harvard Business Review*, October 2004, http://harvardbusinessonline.hbsp.harvard.edu/b01/en/common/item_detail.jhtml?id=R0410D&referral=2340

Truth 5: Marketing and Advertising Can Kill Your Brand

Page

87/88   "A survey of 1,000 consumers . . ." Suzanne Vranica, "Aflac Partly Muzzles Iconic Duck," *Wall Street Journal*, December 2, 2004, http://online.wsj.com/.

214

89/90 "The following are some headlines ..." The headlines were found in the following:

- Jeremy W. Peters, "After Autos' Big Summer, Sales Continue to Weaken," *New York Times*, December 2, 2005.

- "GM to End 401(k) Match," *Rochester Democrat & Chronicle*, December 16, 2005.

- Jathon Sapsford, Joseph B. White, and Dennis K. Berman, "GM Shares Sink to 23-Year Low As Woes Mount," *Wall Street Journal*, December 21, 2005.

- "Toyota Could Make GM No. 2 in 2006," *Rochester Democrat & Chronicle*, December 21, 2005.

Truth 6: Behaviors and Experiences Make the Invisible Visible

Page

98 "Guess who the following core values ..." Enron Corporation, *Enron Annual Report 2000*, Annual Report, 2001.

107 "As Joseph Pine II and James H. Gilmore state in their book ..." Joseph Pine II and James H. Gilmore, *The Experience Economy: Work is Theatre & Every Business a Stage* (Boston, MA: Harvard Business School Press, 1999).

108 "Pine and Gilmore seem to share a similar belief about ..." James H. Gilmore and B. Joseph Pine II, *The Experience IS the Marketing* (Aurora, OH: Strategic Horizons LLP, March 12, 2002).

Truth 7: Employees Are NOT Your Greatest Asset

Page

127/128 "There you will find companies who believe the rhetoric ..." information was found in the following:

- Wegmans Food Markets, "Wegmans Food Markets, Inc.: An Overview," http://www.wegmans.com/about/pressRoom/ overview.asp (accessed April 06, 2007).

- The Container Store, "Learn About Us," http://www. containerstore.com/learn/index.jhtml (accessed April 06, 2007).

134-136 "In his article . . ." Keith H. Hammonds, "Why We Hate HR," *Fast Company*, no. 97 (August 2005): 40.

140 "Consider the cost of a bad hire . . ." Brad Smart and Geoff Smart, *Topgrading: How to Hire, Coach, and Keep A Players* (Pritchett, 2005).

Truth 8: Gaining Buy-in Is the Only Way to Execute a Brand Strategy

Page

148 "A 1999 *Fortune* article . . ." Robert S. Kaplan and David P. Norton, *The Strategy-Focused Organization: How Balanced Scorecard Companies Thrive in the New Business Environment* (Harvard Business School Publishing Corporation, 2001).

152/153 "John Kotter, a Harvard business professor . . ." John P. Kotter, *The Heart of Change* (Boston, MA: Harvard Business School Press, 2002).

153 "Covey claims . . ." Stephen R. Covey, *The 8th Habit: From Effectiveness to Greatness* (New York: Free Press, 2004).

156 "Coming up with the mission statement is simple . . ." Jeffrey Abrahams, *The Mission Statement Book: 301 Corporate Mission Statements From America's Top Companies* (Berkely, CA: Ten Speed Press, 1999).

162 "Remember John Kotter's quote . . ." John P. Kotter, *The Heart of Change* (Boston, MA: Harvard Business School Press, 2002).

172 "As I said earlier, Southwest Airlines . . ." Andrew C. Inkpen and Valerie DeGroot, "Southwest Airlines 2005," Thunderbird, The Garvin School of International Management, 2005.

Truth 9: Most Companies Suck at Capturing Successes and Recognizing People

Page

182 "Yes, I mean good work, not just great . . ." Jim Collins, *Good to Great* (New York: Harper Collins, 2001).

185   "According to a global study . . ." Towers Perrin HR Services,
        Winning Strategies for a Global Workforce: Attracting, Retaining and
        Engaging Employees for Competitive Advantage, Executive Report,
        2006.

185/186 "Here are some facts to back up my claim . . ." Statistics were found
        in the following:

        • Hudson Highland Group, "Most Workers Content with
          Compensation Package, Yet Many Yearn for Flexible Schedules:
          Hudson Survey of 10,000 Reveals Trends in Pay, Health &
          Retirement plans, and Non-Traditional Benefits," press release,
          May 17, 2006.

        • Gallup, "Gallup Study Indicates Actively Disengaged Workers Cost
          U.S. Hundreds of Billions Each Year," *Gallup Management Journal,*
          March 19, 2001, http://gmj.gallup.com/.

        • Michael Cox and Michael E. Rock, *Seven Pillars of Leadership*
          (Toronto: Dryden, 1997): 10-13, quoted in Richard Barrett,
          Liberating the Corporate Soul: Building a Visionary Organization
          (Boston: Butterworth-Heinemann, 1998), 43.

        • CareerBuilder.com, *CareerBuilder.com's Job Forecast: Q1 2006,*
          Quarterly Report, January 2006.

186   "In a recent survey by Salary.com . . ." John Macintyre, "Facts,"
        Southwest Airlines Spirit (November, 2005).

187   "This is supported by . . ." Tom Rath and Donald O. Clifton, *How Full
        Is Your Bucket: Positive Strategies for Work and Life* (New York: Gallup
        Press, 2004).

193   "Mercer Human Resource Consulting estimates . . ." Erin White,
        "Theory & Practice: Praise From Peers Goes a Long Way," *Wall Street
        Journal,* December 19, 2005, http://www.online.wsj.com/public/us/.

202   "Don't forget how much a mis-hire . . ." Brad Smart and Geoff Smart,
        Topgrading: How to Hire, Coach, and Keep A Players (Pritchett, 2005).

Index

A

Accountability: Brand Leadership Council, 110; Brand Lens and sales, 202; brand strategy, 96, 106, 211; culture branding, 43–44; egos and internal politics, 168–69, 212; employee, 13–15, 30, 44, 59, 115, 198–99, 202; Human Resources, 135–44; leadership team, 72, 110, 115, 152, 164, 173, 178, 212; managers, 173, 211; peer-peer, 198; performance benchmarks, 159–60; experiences, 110, 122; template for assigning, 34. See also performance evaluations

Achieving Brand Integrity Performance Success program, 173–76, 175fig

Advertising: agencies, 78–83, 85–93; communication branding, 42; money wasted on, 4–6, 26; Truth #3, 83; Truth #5, 4, 112; tuned-out customers, 85–93. See also brand strategy; marketing

Aflac Duck, 87–88

Ambassadors, 24, 43, 72, 93, 202

Apple, 41

Aspirational brand concept, 100

Attitude: Attitude and Profitability Grid, 138–39; beliefs and, 3–4, 30, 66, 102–103, 154, 168; brand strategy, 115; motivation, 212; poor, 102; positive, 138–39, 138fig, 170, 170fig

B

Behaviors: awareness vs. purchasing, 86; beliefs and, 30, 152, 162–63; brand, recognizing, 158–61; brand-driven, 101–108, 151–61; brand strategy and, 171–78; measurable, 13, 106, 200; recognition and reward, 158–61. See also work culture

Beliefs: Attitude and Profitability Grid, 138–39; attitudes and, 3–4, 30, 66, 102–103, 154, 168; behaviors and, 30, 152, 162–63; brand concept, 57, 100, 102–106, 114–17, 120, 145, 155–56; communicating, 208; cultural change and, 30; customer service, 30, 102, 105; non-aligned, 212; uncovering, 208

BMW, 84

Brand: ambassadors, 24, 43, 72, 93, 202; attributes and associations, 5, 39–40, 50–51, 58, 126–27; behaviors and strategy, 171–78; competitive strengths, 51, 58; concepts, 31, 150–52; concerns and weakness, 52, 58; customer definition, 19; customer experience, 26–27; customer response, 24–25; definition for masses, 19; drivers, 150; employee definition, 19; employee delivered experience, 32, 70, 110; as the employees, 126–27, 154; invisible, 101, 103–104, 153–54; "living the brand," 105, 195–96, 199–202; logo vs., 23; loyalty, 16, 97; operationalizing, 106, 116–17; as "playing field of business," 23; strength, 16; visible, 106, 117,

153–54; work culture, 29–32, 52, 59, 69, 97, 114–15, 115fig, 178. See also brand image; Brand Integrity; buy-in

Brand Charter, 141

Brand image: Brand Integrity Desired Outcome Methodology, 59–63; customer assessment, 51–53, 57; defined by people, 51–52; discovering, 52; employee assessment, 50, 57–59, 119; Truth #3, 83

Brand Integrity: brand image philosophy, 149; Brand Integrity Desired Outcome Methodology, 59–63, 63fig; Brand Lens concept, 99–100, 99fig; at Buckman's, 12–15; buy-in, 149, 168; consistency is key, 27–28, 30, 40; definition, 3; by doing vs. saying, 149; path to achieve, 42–45, 44fig; performance success program, 173–75; Success Story process, 195–97; Truth #6, 93. See also recognition and reward

Brand Integrity Desired Outcome Methodology, 59–63

Brand Lens concept: building, 99–101, 99fig, 116–17, 164; buy-in, 163; goal alignment, 202; Hiring Scorecard, 143–44; invisibility of, 101; performance evaluation, 173–75; recruitment behavior, 203

Brand Match hiring process, 139–144

Brand Stewards, 161, 200

Brand strategy: accountability, 13–14, 96, 106, 211; attributes, unique company, 38–40; behavioral expectations, 13; "being different," 36–47; brand as the business, 22–23; brand image assessments, 57–59, 119; Brand Integrity Desired Outcome Methodology, 59–63; brand position, 71; Brand Stewards, 161, 200; brand team, 96; business objectives, 32–34; business results, 69; Closing the Performance Gap, 161; company heritage, 46; competition, 17, 19, 29, 38–40, 45, 50, 198; consistency, 7, 25–29, 32; customer experience, 70–71; customer outcomes, 59–63; customer tuned-out, 85—86; customers, marketing to, 72–73; customers, target, 70; customer's job, 53–55; customers thoughts, 50; definition, 19–20; Desired Outcome Methodology, 54–55; differentiation, 38, 41–42; elements of, 16; employee experience, 70–71; Employer Brand, building, 132–34; Excellent Customer Service, 102, 105; Experience Audit, 117–18; experiences delivering results, 107–113; experiences vs. logos, 23–25; experiential expectations, 13; experiential judgments, 21; good vs. great company, 28–29, 32; initiatives, implementing, 71–72; "living the brand," 105, 174, 195–96, 199–201; Making the Invisible Visible, 104, 104fig, 123, 153–54; marketing, irresponsible, 80–83; marketing, responsible, 83–85; marketing experiences, 108; Path to Achieve Brand Integrity, 44–47; people (human capital), 29; perceptions, managed, 15, 16; performance-based culture, 15, 66, 161–67, 198; performance management, 158–60; performance objectives, 1, 13, 32–33, 107, 176, 194; personalizing for employees, 154; points of difference, 6, 42, 45–47, 61–63, 63fig, 89; process improvement, 29; product placement,

219

Customer experience: benefits being sought, 102; brand image assessment, 51, 57; branding, 26–27, 43–44, 106; buying decisions, 26; Chief Experience Officer, 110; competitive advantage, 17; employee behaviors, 24, 25, 28, 52, 57; employee recognition, 192; employees, star, 129; employees performance, 130–31; identifying desired, 29; managing, 102; perceptions, managed, 15; post-purchase, 113; pre-purchase, 111–12; purchase, 112–13; relationship building, 114; tune-out by, 85–86; understanding, 70–71; what they think, 50

D

Daytime Vacation Spot, 40

Deloitte Technology Fast 500 List, 209

Dilbert cartoon, 87, 148

E

Employee: A-players, 138–40, 138fig, 160; accountability, 13–15, 30, 43, 44, 115, 198–99, 202; actionable strategy, focused, 5; Attitude and Profitability Grid, 138–39, 138fig; as brand, 126–27, 132–34; Brand Charter, 141; brand concepts, understanding, 51, 57, 150–52; buy-in, 155–57, 169–70, 170fig, 200–201; communication, 136, 209; disengaged, 184–87; ego, non-aligned, 66, 67, 168–69, 212; engagement, increasing, 197; Experience Scorecard, 136–38; as "greatest asset," 127–29; high potential, 22; interactions impact brand, 22; "living the brand," 105, 195–96, 199–201; loyalty, 16, 59, 97, 107, 187; money-motivated, 190–92; not satisfied, 185; performance, 128–31, 205; performance mind-set, 163, 198; personal fulfillment, 186–87; productivity, increasing, 197; referrals, 59, 170; self-assessments, 115, 141, 164; Truth #6, 13. See also behaviors; beliefs; performance evaluations

Employer Brand, 132–34

Energizer Bunny, 88

Engagement in process principle, 157

Excellent Customer Service, 102, 105

Expectation clarity principle, 157

Experience Audit, 117–18, 118

The Experience Economy (Pine and Gilmore), 107–108

Experience Scorecard, 136–38

F

Fast Company Magazine, 20

G

Gieco, 84

General Motors, 89–93

Good to Great (Collins), 182–83

H

Hammond, Keith, 134, 136

Hay Group, 134–35

Hiring Scorecard, 142–44

Human resources: assessments, brand-behavior, 43; assessments, brand-image, 57–59, 119; Brand Charter, 141; Brand Competencies and Behaviors, 159; Brand Lens concept, 203; Brand Match hiring process, 139–144; employee orientation, 43, 139, 141, 203; high potential performers, 22; Hiring Scorecard, 142–44; job profiles, 99, 161; recognition and reward, 158, 160–61; self-assessments, employee, 115, 141, 164; talent management, 16, 134–43. See also performance evaluations; recognition and reward

I

"I Caught You Living the Brand" recognition, 199–202

Investigating Reality Interview, 66–75

J

JetBlue, 171–72

JetBlue Airlines, 41

Jones, Jerry, 41

L

Leadership team: accountability, 110, 115, 122, 135, 152, 159, 164, 168, 173, 178, 212; Attitude and Profitability Grid, 138–39, 138fig; behaviors, employees and brand, 105; brand concept development, 98–99, 105; brand-driven business, 106; Brand Leadership Council, 110; business results, 69, 103; buy-in, barrier to, 167–69; buy-in role, 163–65, 175fig; CEO (Chief Experience Officer), 110; egos, non-aligned, 67, 168–69, 212; experience audit, 117–18; Experience Scorecard, 136–38, 138fig; invisible brand, 103–104; mediocre employees, 128, 130–31; mission statements, 156–57; objectives for, 164–65; people and processes, aligning, 208–12; performance mind-set, 163, 198; poor performance, managing, 176–78; power types, 210–12; questions for, 66–75; strategy implementation, 148–49; success stories, 182; talent management, 134–43; teamwork, fostering, 204. See also Brand Integrity; Brand Lens concept; performance evaluations; recognition and reward

Loyalty, 16, 59, 97, 107, 187

M

Making the Invisible Visible, 104, 104fig, 123, 153–54

Marketing: brand strategy vs., 29; branding experiences vs., 23–27; customers as marketing department, 112; to customers effectively, 72–74; helping customers, 55; ineffective, 4–6, 21, 26, 29, 78–93; irresponsible, 80–83; responsible, 83–85. See also advertising; brand strategy

Mercer Human Resources Consulting, 193

Morton Salt, 18

O

"Obsessive Branding Disorder" (Fast Company), 20

Operational procedures and policies, 16, 59

Organizational branding, 5, 6

Outback Steakhouse, 41

P

PAETEC Communications, 209–210

Partner relationships, 16

Path to Achieve Brand Integrity, 44–47

Perception, 12

Performance evaluations: accountability, employee, 59; Achieving Brand Integrity Performance Success program, 173–76, 175fig; brand behavior evaluation, 43; brand concepts, 99, 173; brand integrity, 173–75; Brand Lens concept, 173–75; brand strategy, 158–60; branded experiences, 115; fairness vs. unfairness, 134–35; legal objective, 129; performance benchmarks, 159–60; performance gap, 176–78; performance objectives, 1, 13, 32–33, 107, 176, 194

Point of Difference Opportunity Grid, 61–63, 63fig

Post-purchase touchpoints, 113

Pre-purchase touchpoints, 111–12

Price-to-entry brand concept, 100

Product branding, 5

Product development, 16

Professional service firm touchpoints, 113–14

Trout, Jack, 168

Truth #1, 10–34, 97, 106

Truth #2, 36–47

Truth #3, 48–63, 83

Truth #4, 64–74

Truth #5, 4, 76–93, 112

Truth #6, 13, 20, 30, 93, 94–123, 96, 135, 141, 153

Truth #7, 124–45, 194

Truth #8, 9, 98, 99, 135, 141, 146–78, 200

Truth #9, 160, 178, 179, 180–205

Truth #10, 206–212

V

Values-based brand concept, 100

Vendor relationships, 16

W

Web sites, 43; accountability template, 34; Achieving Brand Integrity Performance Success program, 176; Brand Competencies and Behaviors, 159; Brand Integrity Success Story, 197; Brand Lens exercises, 117; brand value assessment, 59; brandintegrity.com, 7; business objectives guide, 34; Celebrating Success Workshops, 201; Experience Audit, 118; Experience Scorecard, 137; Hiring Scorecard, 144; Investigating Reality Interview, 75; outcomes, customers' desired, 63; Path to Achieve Brand Integrity, 45; Points of Difference questions, 45; Stage Experience Prioritization, 122

Wegmans, 128

Witnesses, 161, 200

Work culture: brand-driven, 29–32, 52, 59, 69, 97, 114–15, 115fig, 178; performance-based, 15, 161–67, 198; personal fulfillment, 186–87

X

Xerox, 86